SPIRITUAL DESIRE

LEGACY
PUBLISHERS INTERNATIONAL

SPIRITUAL DESIRE

Darlene Bishop

Unless otherwise indicated, all Scripture quotations are from the *King James Version* of the Bible. Definitions marked *"Strong's"* are from *Strong's Exhaustive Concordance of the Bible,* Dugan Publishers, Inc., Gordonsville, Tennessee.

SPIRITUAL DESIRE

ISBN 1-880809-52-4

Printed in the United States of America
Copyright © 2005—by Darlene Bishop

Legacy Publishers International
1301 South Clinton Street
Denver, CO 80247
Phone: 303-283-7480 FAX: 303-283-7536

Library of Congress Cataloging-in-Publication Data Pending

1 2 3 4 5 6 7 8 9 / 09 08 07 06 05

DEDICATION

To my mother, who has now gone on to be with the Lord. She taught me the importance of prayer and how to go about it.

CONTENTS

Therefore I say unto you, What things soever ye DESIRE, when ye pray, believe that ye receive them, and ye shall have them.

Mark 11:24

INTRODUCTION

Desire is a strange thing. When God uses it, it's wonderful. But when the devil takes hold of it, the results are inevitably tragic. We need strong desires in our lives, but we need to make sure what the source of those desires is and who is controlling them.

One morning I was in prayer. I was asking the Lord to help me bring my every thought under subjection to Him. I wanted to have His mind and to think His thoughts, so that His river could flow out through me more forcefully. As I prayed, the Lord showed me that when the devil gives us a thought, and that thought becomes a desire within us, we're in trouble. But when God gives us a thought, and that thought becomes a desire within us, then the devil's in trouble.

When the Lord puts something into our spirit, it takes hold of us and becomes a powerful force that can transform our lives for good. More of us need God-inspired desire. When the enemy puts something into our spirit, it too takes hold of us and becomes a powerful force for destruction. May God save us from this fate.

Spiritual Desire

The intensity of our spiritual desire determines not only our present lot in life, but also our future destiny. Desire determines our effectiveness in prayer, our intensity in worship, and the depth of our personal relationship with God. What could possibly be more important?

"But don't all Christians have spiritual desire?" some might ask. As a matter of fact, no, they don't. Through the years, I've noticed that new Christians are full of spiritual desire, and that desire drives them to seek God in every possible way. Then, as time goes on, their spiritual desire seems to wane and is replaced with fleshly desires, leaving them with a form of spirituality that is highly offensive to God. They have clearly lost their "first love."

This is not only sad; it's dangerous. A loss of desire causes people to become careless with their personal testimonies and to slack off in other important ways. This, in turn, often leads them to backsliding and a resultant loss of everything they have worked for in God. Is desire that important a factor? Oh yes, without desire nothing will be accomplished in God.

It's time to let God put a new burning zeal within our spirits to be all that He has called us to be and to do all that He has called us to do. If revival is to come to the church as a whole, many things have to change. Our temples must be cleansed. There must come a return of the separation God calls for between His people and the world, and men and women of God must again have Him as their source of all things. All of this requires desire on our part. In short, there is an inescapable link between desire and destiny.

If you're hungry for God, please read on.

Darlene Bishop
Solid Rock Church
Monroe, Ohio

Chapter 1

NEEDED: MEN AND WOMEN OF DESIRE

And Caleb said, He that smiteth Kirjathsepher, and taketh it, to him will I give Achsah my daughter to wife. And Othniel the son of Kenaz, Caleb's younger brother, took it: and he gave him Achsah his daughter to wife. And it came to pass, when she came to him, that she moved him to ask of her father a field: and she lighted from off her ass; and Caleb said unto her, What wilt thou? And she said unto him, Give me a blessing: for thou hast given me a south land; give me also springs of water. And Caleb gave her the upper springs and the nether springs.

Judges 1:12-15

This man Caleb was, many believe, Moses' brother-in-law. He was a mighty warrior in his own right, and he fought and won many battles for Israel over a period of some eighty-three years. More importantly, he was a man who knew something about desire.

After Caleb had helped other tribes to receive their inheritance in the promised land, he felt that it was his turn. He declared:

Now therefore give me this mountain ... .

Joshua 14:12

It didn't matter to Caleb that the land of which he spoke was infested with giants. He had known for years that he was *"well able to overcome"* them (Numbers 13:30). And he did. He expelled all the giants, the sons of Anak who were then living in the land, and the land became part of his permanent inheritance.

Caleb was also given the land of Hebron as part of his inheritance, but there was still another land that he desired. It had once been known as Kirjathsepher, but the name had been changed to Debir.

For some reason, Caleb didn't want to go out and fight to take this particular land. Perhaps he was tired of fighting by then. Whatever the reason, he now advertised for someone to do battle for him—for a price. In a sense, he put an ad in the local paper saying that if someone would take this land for him, he would give them, in return, his daughter Achsah in marriage. Not a bad deal!

The ad was answered by Caleb's own nephew, a young man named Othniel. Othniel took up the challenge, and he was able to win the city in question for Caleb. And when he did, his uncle, always good to his word, gave Othniel his daughter in marriage.

ACHSAH'S DESIRE

As a wedding gift, Caleb gave his daughter some land described in the Bible as *"a south land."* Strangely, she wasn't satisfied with this gift. Apparently the land in question was dry, for the daughter now asked Caleb to give her some source of water, some *"springs"* so that she could irrigate the land.

Achsah was wise enough to know that dry land would not produce a suitable livelihood for her and her family. "Daddy," she urged. "Thank you for the land, but there's something else I need. Could you give me some springs to water it?" This request didn't anger Caleb in the least. He loved his daughter and wanted her to have the best of everything. If she needed a spring, he wanted her to have a spring. His response was to give her even more than she had requested. He gave her two groups of springs: *"the upper springs and the nether springs."* That's just like our God. He always gives us more than we request, to show us His great love.

But does this nice little story have anything to do with us today in the twenty-first century? Oh, it has everything to do with us. Nothing is accomplished in God's kingdom without desire. Desire is the very bedrock of our faith. Without a "want to," you will never do anything in the Spirit realm.

In the story, everyone had a desire. Caleb wanted the place known as Debir, Othniel wanted Achsah as his wife, and she wanted some springs to water her land and make it fruitful. In the end, everyone got what they wanted. That's how powerful a force desire is.

3

Desire Makes Men Do Strange Things:

Othniel was not the first man who was willing to face giants to have the woman he loved, and Achsah was not the first woman to bring the best out in her man. Desire is a powerful tool.

When I was attending high school, I never had lunch money to eat with the other students, so as often as I could, I would run home, fix myself a quick sandwich, and try to eat it and get back to school before our thirty-minute lunch break was over. One day, as I was home preparing myself a sandwich, I noticed that Daddy was in the backyard splitting wood for the fireplace with an axe. There was a young man with him.

I knew Lawrence Bishop, and we had spoken to each other on occasion, but just in passing. Now, for some reason, Lawrence had stopped by unannounced. He suddenly took the axe from my father's hands and began to put on a show that I was sure was staged just for me. My, how he chopped wood that day!

It's wonderful when we women have the ability to bring out the best in our man. Lawrence never split wood by hand again, but he did a wonderful job of it that day. This was the beginning of a deeper relationship that would lead us to marriage within about six months.

We're not told exactly what Othniel had to do to win his bride or just how difficult it was. He must have fought some terrible battles. But whatever the price he paid, afterward the victory was sweet. He now had a wife, his father-in-law was a wealthy landowner, and he had given them land and springs to water that land. But it all came because of his deep desire.

WHAT IS DESIRE? AND WHY IS IT SO POWERFUL?

Webster's Dictionary defines desire in this way: "A wish or longing; a request or petition; the object of longing" Desire is not just an inclination to want; it's a force to be reckoned with. It is a boiling, passionate zeal. It's not just a whimsical fancy, as some might imagine; it's an overwhelming compulsion. Jesus said:

> *Therefore I say unto you, What things soever ye DESIRE, when ye pray, believe that ye receive them, and ye shall have them.*

> Mark 11:24

Whatever we desire we can have. Still, many of us dare to go to the house of God without desire, and once there, we dare to utter prayers that are little more than momentary wishes, flashes in the mind. Usually, before we have left the church building, we've already forgotten what we prayed about that day. Whatever it was, it didn't captivate our souls.

Whatever we desire we can have.

This current generation doesn't seem to be very desirous of the things of God. Perhaps it's because their desire has been turned to the flesh. This, of course, is dangerous. Paul wrote to the Ephesians:

> *Among whom also we all had our conversation in times past in the lusts of our flesh, fulfilling the desires of the flesh and of the mind; and were by nature the children of wrath, even as others.*

> Ephesians 2:3

All of us were guilty of feeding the desires of the flesh before we came to know Christ. But after we are already His, there are things that clearly should not be cultivated and nurtured in our lives. They are *"desires of the flesh and of the mind,"* and fulfilling them will cause us to lose many of the spiritual battles we face. How can we be victorious in the things of the Spirit if we're too busy fulfilling the desires of the flesh?

What is your desire? What do you seek after with fervent, boiling zeal? The reason many get old before their time is that they have lost their spiritual desire. Once this happens, you might as well start picking out your tombstone. If you have no more desire, you've lost everything.

One of the things most affected by a loss of spiritual desire is our prayer life. We will be examining this subject in more detail in later chapters, but suffice it to say here that it's not enough just to pray. We have to pray out of true desire. Let's take another look at what Jesus said in Mark 11:24:

> *Therefore I say unto you, What things soever ye DESIRE, when ye pray, believe that ye receive them, and ye shall have them.*
>
> Mark 11:24

We usually emphasize the need for faith with our prayers, and this is an important element, but desire is clearly just as important. If there's no desire, why pray in the first place? The reason your prayers are not being answered may be the lack of any fervent, boiling, zeal behind them.

For instance, if I ask a crowd of Christians how many of them want spiritual gifts to operate in their lives, every hand in the house goes up. But if that's true, why don't they have them? Could it be because they don't have a fervent, boiling, zeal for them, a compelling desire that would not let them rest until they had them in place?

Oh, yes, people say, "I'd love to have the gift of healing," but then they're in such a hurry to get out of the service and go somewhere to eat that they don't have time to wait for the prayer around the altar. That speaks louder than their words.

We sometimes think we desire something, but do we really? One day I said to someone, "I've always wanted to be able to play the piano."

"Well, did you ever take any lessons?" they asked.

That question hit me like a ton of bricks, and suddenly I realized how foolish my statement had been. "No," I had to admit. "I guess I didn't want to play as much as I thought I did." If I had wanted to play, I would have been asking someone who knew how to play to teach me.

What we call vision is often nothing more than a desire planted in our hearts by the Lord. One of our favorite Bible statements is this:

Where there is no vision, the people perish.

Proverbs 29:18

What sort of vision does this verse speak of? Is this the kind of vision in which you're knocked to the floor and you see a motion picture on the back of your eyelids? No, this reference to *"vision"* means that you have a certain goal, or desire, ever before you. When you have such a vision, you think about it and talk about it constantly, and you pray about it until it becomes a reality.

Revival, or spiritual renewal, often begins with one person's vision, one person's spiritual desire. This is a transforming force.

A CRIPPLED MAN'S DESIRE

In Jesus' time, there was a pool in Jerusalem known as the Pool of Bethesda. It had huge porches where the sick gathered because something very unusual took place there periodically. Once each year the angel of the Lord would go down and trouble the water of that pool. When this happened, the first person to get into the water that was thus troubled would be healed.

One particular man had been going to the pool for many years. For thirty-eight years, since the time of his youth, he had been crippled, and he hoped to be healed through this miracle occurring at the pool. Each time, however, when he tried to get into the water when the moment for healing came, others were able to get there before him. They were healed, and he was not, and again he was disappointed.

Revival, or spiritual renewal, often begins with one person's vision, one person's spiritual desire.

In the early years of his attempts, he had no doubt been excited about the prospects of being healed. "This may be the day," he must have told himself. But days passed, and weeks, and then months and years, and he was still lying there in the same condition. But something was about to change for him.

One day Jesus passed by the Pool of Bethesda. He saw the man who had been sitting in the same place for so long, and He asked him a rather amazing question:

Wilt thou be made whole?

John 5:6

It seems like a ridiculous question to ask a person who's been lying at the same place for many years in hopes of being healed, but when we examine the context, the question was not ridiculous at all. The crippled man had somehow lost his expectation, and his desire had dwindled. Unless he could change his desire, his situation wouldn't change either.

He had been coming to the Pool of Bethesda for so long that he forgot why he had come in the first place. His visit there had become a way of life rather than a portal into a new one. Jesus was there to remind him of his purpose and destiny, to stir up his desire once again.

What this man experienced in the physical is so common among Christians today. When we're newly saved, we go to church with great desire and expectation. There are so many things we want and want desperately. We want to be filled with the Holy Ghost. We want to have gifts that will make us useful in the church. We want to do something concrete, like become an usher or a Sunday school teacher. But sometimes it seems that God is using everybody else but us, so we decide to just sit down for a while and be a "normal" church member.

When this happens, it represents a loss of desire on our part, and what follows is a tragedy. All too soon, our youth passes, and we suddenly find ourselves much older, but still we've not done anything of substance for the Lord.

When Jesus asked the man this question, the man had an answer, and most of us would think it was a good one:

Sir, I have no man, when the water is troubled, to put me into the pool: but while I am coming, another step-peth down before me.

John 5:7

This gentleman had no one to help him. People had failed him, so he had given up the hope of ever receiving his miracle.

9

The Loss of Hope:

The loss of hope is always a terrible thing. The writer of the Proverbs said:

Hope deferred maketh the heart sick.

Proverbs 13:12

Anytime you lose hope, your heart becomes sick. There is another part to this verse, and it's very powerful. It says:

But when the desire cometh, it is a tree of life.

Proverbs 13:12

This refers to the tree of life that was situated in the midst of the garden of Eden and represented everything mankind needed to live an abundant life. That's how powerful desire is. Hope that is deferred makes you sick, but desire will rejuvenate you. It will give you a reason to jump out of bed every morning, a reason to comb your hair, get dressed, and get out of the house to see what the day holds for you.

Thank God for that. There are far too many people who are confined to their homes these days, and their life consists of soap operas and junk magazines. How good it is to be out and about for the kingdom of God! How good it is to feel useful in this world! How good it is to have destiny and purpose!

After Proverbs 13 speaks of *"hope deferred"* making the soul sick and desire providing *"a tree of life,"* it goes on to make another wonderful statement about the importance of desire:

The desire accomplished is sweet to the soul.

Proverbs 13:19

What more needs to be said? It's time to stir up our spiritual desire.

FOUR FRIENDS AND THEIR DESIRE

One day Jesus was preaching in a house in Capernaum, and four men came bearing a litter with a sick friend on it. They had heard it said that everyone whom Jesus touched was healed, and they were determined to get their friend to Him.

But, alas, when they got there, all of the handicapped parking spaces were taken, and the fire marshal had declared the meeting at full capacity and closed the doors. There was no way to get their friend inside.

Most of us would have decided about then that it must not have been God's will to heal the man, but these four men were different. They had a burning desire that would not be denied. They could not give up that easily, and they began looking for some other way to get the task accomplished.

Eventually they decided to take the man up onto the roof and lower him down to Jesus. Where did they get the ladder to get up there and the tools they needed to take the roof apart? We don't know. What we do know is that they did whatever was necessary to get it done. Desire always finds a way.

When you have a desire to do something for God, there are not enough demons in hell to stop you. If God has called you to preach, someone may refuse to recognize your calling and give you an opportunity. But if you have a burning desire to do it anyway, you'll find some place to preach—even if it's on some busy street corner. As the old saying goes, "Where there's a will, there's a way."

Real desire is overwhelming and causes you to say, "I've simply got to have it! I'm going to get it! And nothing and no one will stop me!" Do you still have that kind of spiritual desire?

JACOB'S DESIRE

When Jacob had wrestled with the angel of the Lord for hours already, he must have been exhausted. Still, he wouldn't let go. He said:

I will not let thee go, except thou bless me.

Genesis 32:26

Jacob wanted what rightfully belonged to him, and he refused to give up until it was his. It didn't matter that his hip had come out of joint, and that he would have to limp the rest of his life. He was determined to fight for what he wanted. And he got it.

When I was first saved, I remember the older people in the church standing to testify and turning to point at the section where we young people were sitting. "Honey," they would say, "if you want to receive the Holy Ghost, you have to want it more than anything else. You have to want it more than you want a boyfriend or girlfriend." I didn't know much about the Holy Ghost baptism, but I knew that I wanted it, and those of us who wanted it badly enough received this wonderful experience and the power it provided.

It's very sad to me that the older people among us today can't say much to our younger generation. Our young people seem to already know it all. But that's another story. This book is about desire.

Some Christians haven't desired anything more than fleshly comforts in a very long time. Prayer is a chore for them because they don't have strong spiritual desires. When you want something from God, you can't wait to get into His presence. Your desire makes all the difference in the world.

THE WOMAN OF CANAAN AND HER DESIRE

Years ago, when I read the story of the woman of Canaan who approached Jesus, I couldn't understand it. This woman came to the Lord and told Him that her daughter was *"grievously vexed with a devil"* (Matthew 15:22), but His response and that of His disciples was very unusual:

> *But he answered her not a word. And his disciples came and besought him, saying, Send her away; for she crieth after us.*
>
> Matthew 15:23

Why would Jesus ignore a woman who was seeking His help? And why would the disciples try to send her away? That was humiliating.

Jesus explained His actions this way:

> *He answered and said, I am not sent but unto the lost sheep of the house of Israel.*
>
> Matthew 15:24

When the woman didn't seem to be dissuaded by this response, Jesus answered her further, making His position very clear:

> *But he answered and said, It is not meet to take the children's bread, and to cast it to dogs.*
>
> Matthew 15:26

13

That was about as harsh as anyone could be, and still this woman was not turned away by Jesus' words. He had first ignored her, and the disciples had tried to send her away. Then He had told her plainly that He was only sent to *the lost sheep of the house of Israel.*" When all of that hadn't worked, He told her that it was not right to take *"the children's bread"* and give it to *"dogs."*

Amazingly, this woman pressed on, and what she said next touched the heart of Jesus:

And she said, Truth, Lord: yet the dogs eat of the crumbs which fall from their masters' table.

Matthew 15:27

With desire like that, who could be stopped? Jesus' next response to this woman of Canaan has amazed men and women in every generation:

Then Jesus answered and said unto her, O woman, great is thy faith: be it unto thee even as thou wilt.

Matthew 15:28

Because of the intensity of her desire, this woman received what she wanted:

And her daughter was made whole from that very hour.

Matthew 15:28

In all of this, God was just testing her desire. If she truly had desire, nothing could stop her. But if she didn't have desire, nothing that He could do would help her. She was willing to receive just *"the crumbs"* because she knew that it was enough. Consequently, this woman had her desire accomplished. Her demon-possessed daughter was delivered.

True desire simply will not be denied. It will move the hand of God every time. It will deliver your children from sin, and it will bring healing to your sick body. It's time to pray for renewed spiritual desire, for having it will surely turn your life upside down.

> *True desire simply will not be denied. It will move the hand of God every time.*

BARTIMAEUS' DESIRE

Another wonderful biblical example of these truths about the power of spiritual desire is that of the blind man named Bartimaeus. He was sitting by the roadside begging one day when he heard the approach of many people. He asked someone what was going on, and they told him that Jesus of Nazareth was passing that way. When Bartimaeus heard this news, he began to cry out:

Jesus, thou Son of David, have mercy on me.

Mark 10:47

Many people tried to silence Bartimaeus that day, but he refused to be silenced. Instead, he cried out even louder. The Scriptures say of him:

But he cried the more a great deal.

Mark 10:48

Eventually, Jesus couldn't help but notice this persistent and determined man. "Bring that man who has such great desire," He must have said. "I cannot pass by without healing him."

I can somehow picture Bartimaeus that day, getting up and stumbling his way through the crowd. People pushed him aside, but that didn't stop him. They tried to hush him up, but that didn't stop him. He knew that he somehow needed to get Jesus' attention if he was to receive his miracle, and he desperately wanted to be healed. That desire would not allow him to give way to any hindrance. He must persist, and he did.

It's interesting to note that Bartimaeus got Jesus' attention by making enough noise. Yet the trend in our modern churches is for all of us to maintain silence in the services. How can this be right? When people go to a ball game, they scream and jump for their favorite team to win. May God help us to have the same desire for spiritual things as we have for the carnal.

When Bartimaeus, a man who had never seen the light of day and had thus spent his entire existence in darkness, stood before Jesus, it took only a simple touch from the Master's hand to bring light flooding into his eyes. Imagine it! The very first thing Bartimaeus saw was the incarnate Son of God standing in front of him. His desire had produced the longed-for result and much more, and from that day onward, Bartimaeus followed Jesus.

All of us could use more of this boiling zeal that comes with real spiritual desire.

NEHEMIAH'S DESIRE

A wonderful biblical example of spiritual desire and what it can accomplish is the story of Nehemiah. This man was a slave captured in Israel and taken to Persia. There, he rose in importance and became a trusted servant of the king. In this capacity, he was doing well ... until one day his world was turned upside down.

When someone told Nehemiah that the holy city of Jerusalem had been looted and burned and that its once regal walls and gates now lay in ruins, the news so disturbed him that he could no longer perform his duties in a proper way. He asked the king for a leave of absence so that he could go back home and try to rebuild the city. Amazingly, this request was granted.

When Nehemiah arrived in Jerusalem, he found the situation to be worse than he had imagined. Not only was the once great city decimated, but it was surrounded by enemies. He gathered the Jewish people remaining in and around the city and told them his plan to rebuild. If they were willing to join him in this task, they would have to work with their trowels in one hand and their weapons in the other. They could do it, he assured them.

Then an astonishing thing happened. Despite their limitations, these people (none of them masons or carpenters by trade) were able to do the needed work in just fifty-two days. Nehemiah's desire built walls and gates and restored the city for the people of Jerusalem. And that's what renewed spiritual desire will do for you too.

For many years, I had a burning desire to build a home for unwed teenage mothers. The burden of it was always in the back of my mind, always nagging at me. Every time I heard someone speaking about the evils of abortion, I knew instinctively that we had to do something about it. We preach against abortion ourselves, but for too long, we offered no alternatives.

That vision never faded until we, at Solid Rock Church, were able to fulfill it. To do so, we had to work with our implements in one hand and our weapons in the other, but we accomplished it. Today our home for unwed mothers, The Darlene Bishop Home for Life, is a reality that is changing many lives.

THE DESIRES OF YOUR HEART

It's all well and good to think of Caleb's desire, or Jacob's desire or Nehemiah's desire, but what about your desire? There's a biblical promise that we all love regarding desire, and it brings this subject down to the personal level, when it says:

Delight thyself also in the Lord; and he shall give THEE the desires of THINE heart. Commit thy way unto the Lord; trust also in him; and he shall bring it to pass.

Psalm 37:4-5

The Lord is committed to giving you the desires of your heart, but He also requires something of you. *"Delight THYSELF in the Lord."* That's your part of the bargain, and it indicates to the Lord your spiritual desire.

To delight in someone means that you experience great pleasure and joy in their presence. So the meaning of this passage is that when you begin to experience great pleasure and joy just by being in God's presence, then whatever you ask Him for will be granted. How wonderful!

Is it dangerous for God to say that He'll give us the desires of our heart? Not at all. It happens because His desire becomes our desire. When we want what He wants, we can have it, and we'll get it. Is what you're asking God for today just a passing fancy, or is your request stimulated by a burning, passionate desire that represents the heart of God? It makes all the difference in the world.

A woman who is praying for her husband to be saved or to otherwise conform to the will of God, must have ignited within her a passionate, flaming desire that will not allow her to rest until her request is granted. When she has her hand on her hus-

18

band in the night, he may think that she's just lovingly stroking him, but in reality, she's saying, "Holy Ghost, get him! Don't let him rest until he's done the right thing. Take away his peace, and don't let his mind find solace until he's made it all right."

She'll not be able to eat without thinking of her husband's salvation. Every time she gets down to pray, she'll want him to be right there beside her. Every time she goes to church, she'll declare, "This is the last time I'll ever have to come without my baby. Thank You, Lord, that he will not go to hell. He is a mighty man of God."

When a woman prays with that intensity of desire, what man could resist? The Bible declares that a man can't help but get saved when a wife goes after his soul with real desire, and the same is true for a believing husband:

For the unbelieving husband is sanctified by the wife, and the unbelieving wife is sanctified by the husband: else were your children unclean; but now are they holy.

1 Corinthians 7:14

That unbelieving spouse will be saved, so don't give up. Keep holding on. Some unbelieving husbands, when they come under the conviction of the Holy Ghost, seem to become "meaner than a junkyard dog," but that just means that the Spirit is nudging them. Hold on. Don't give up. Your victory is coming.

THE POWER OF FLESHLY DESIRE

Othniel wanted a wife, and that desire prompted him to fight giants and overrun a city. And we, too, can have what we want in God—if we really want it badly enough and go after it with fiery zeal. But, as I said in the introduction, Satan, too, utilizes desire. If he can make us Christians want something that we shouldn't have bad enough, he knows that we'll do anything to get it—even risk alienating ourselves from God. Such an overpowering desire is known in scripture as *"the lust of the flesh"*:

> *This I say then, Walk in the Spirit, and ye shall not fulfil the lust of the flesh. For the flesh lusteth against the Spirit, and the Spirit against the flesh: and these are contrary the one to the other: so that ye cannot do the things that ye would.*

Galatians 5:16-17

The sad thing is that most Christians know that the thing they're pursuing will take them straight to hell, but they become so obsessed with it that they're sure they just can't live without it. The results of such a pursuit are always very devastating.

One of King David's sons, Amnon, became obsessed with his half-sister Tamar. He was so sick with desire for her that it drove him to forcibly rape her. Then, when the evil deed was done, he despised Tamar so much that he wanted her out of his sight immediately.

Do you see how Satan works? He convinces you that you need something so badly that you just can't live without it, and then, once you have it, you're sick about it. It didn't bring you the joy you thought it would.

The result was even sadder for Amnon. His mistake cost him his life, and that is the price Satan wants to make you pay for sin as well. As Jesus said to Peter:

> *Simon, Simon, behold, Satan hath desired to have you, that he may sift you as wheat.*

Luke 22:31

Satan wants you so badly that he's willing to do most anything to get you. Put yourself firmly on the side of God's desire.

ALLYING YOURSELF WITH GOD'S DESIRE

That's what David did. He said:

One thing have I desired of the Lord, that will I seek after; that I may dwell in the house of the Lord all the days of my life, to behold the beauty of the Lord, and to inquire in his temple.

Psalm 27:4

What we desire is what we seek after, and because David's desire was toward God, he became *"a man after his own heart"* (1 Samuel 13:14). My mamma always said that you can talk to somebody for ten minutes and know where their heart is. It doesn't take long.

If we are to get anything from God, we first must have a spiritual desire, and if we are to continue being blessed by God, we must not lose that spiritual desire. Fight to maintain it fresh and strong.

I notice the young men and women who gather on the front rows of our churches. They're so fervent that they never miss a service, and they love God so much that they jump higher than anyone else during the worship times. But if they're not careful, they'll gradually lose that fervency.

Such a desire must be cultivated and must lead to our doing something for God and His kingdom. God puts a desire within you, and if you don't do something with it, it will die. And when your desire dies, your spirituality will die with it.

21

I see it all the time. People get saved, and they have a zeal to do something great for God. Then, before long, I see them sitting calmly and quietly like everyone else, satisfied to go though the motions without any real excitement or determination. Oh, please don't lose the fire of your spiritual desire. Keep it ever burning bright, and your future will be just as bright.

Needed: men and women of godly desire. There is an inseparable link between your desire and your destiny.

Chapter 2

DESIRE DETERMINES DESTINY

But without faith it is impossible to please him: for he that cometh to God must believe that he is, and that he is a rewarder of them that diligently seek him.

Hebrews 11:6

What does it mean to diligently seek God? It means that we crave to investigate more about Him. We long to search out His hidden parts. We long to learn to worship Him in new ways. We want what He wants for us.

Our God rewards such desire. The Scriptures declare:

Ask, and it shall be given you; seek, and ye shall find; knock, and it shall be opened unto you: for every one

*that asketh receiveth; and he that seeketh findeth; and
to him that knocketh it shall be opened.*

Matthew 7:7-8

*Blessed are they that keep his testimonies, and that
seek him with the whole heart.*

Psalm 119:2

*The Lord searcheth all hearts, and understandeth all the
imaginations of the thoughts: if thou seek him, he will
be found of thee.*

1 Chronicles 28:9

GOD REWARDS DILIGENCE

God rewards diligence and not slothfulness. Those who do only what is required of them on their job should not be looking for either a raise or a promotion. Far too many people say, "That's not part of my job description." That's okay, but let's see what happens when promotion time comes. Promotion comes to us only when we have become overqualified for our current position.

Some people want to do public ministry, but they don't do a good job with the first simple tasks assigned to them. If you can't be faithful in the nursery, how can you qualify to head up some critical ministry of the church? When you're overqualified for the spot you now occupy, then God will promote you to another division of His kingdom.

My grandson Kane was bored with first grade because he already knew everything being taught. When the time came to graduate from that class, he felt that he was ready to move on to the third grade. Recently, when I was trying to read a book to him, he was finishing the pages ahead of my words and urging me to hurry it up.

When you become overqualified for your current position, you also become dissatisfied and want to move on. Desire moves you up the ladder.

GOD RESPONDS TO HUNGRY HEARTS

The Lord taught us in His Word:

Desire spiritual gifts.

1 Corinthians 14:1

If you don't have spiritual gifts, it may be because you haven't desired them enough. When we go to God, we don't seem to be absolutely sure of what we want from Him. One day it's one thing, and the next day it's something else entirely. But desire keeps us focused. It causes us to say, "I'm not leaving here until I get that. I want that, and I won't stop until it's mine."

We go to bed thinking about it, we wake up thinking about it, and we go through the day thinking about it. We might be driving a car and doing a good job of it, but at the same time, the desire on the inside of us is saying, "I want more of God."

When we truly hunger for God, we get very specific about our desire. In this way, our desire actually determines our destiny, for God responds to hungry people:

Blessed are they which do hunger and thirst after righteousness: for they shall be filled.

Matthew 5:6

This is one of God's inviolable laws. The hunger of a man's soul must be satisfied. That's His commitment. He fills all those who recognize that they have a need. Those who are not hungry need not apply.

David knew this secret. He said:

As the hart panteth after the water brooks, so panteth my soul after thee, O God. My soul thirsteth for God, for the living God.

Psalm 42:1-2

This is the same panting desire of which the writer of Hebrews speaks in Hebrews 11:6. To diligently seek God carries the meaning of experiencing a passion that causes you to breathe hard.

David was panting after God. He simply had to have Him. There was nothing that he wanted more in life. He was king over Israel, so he had plenty of resources at his disposal. He had all the women he could ever want, and yet there was something that drove him forward. This one thing dominated his thinking and motivated his every word and action. He desperately wanted more of God.

GOD NEVER DOES THE UNNECESSARY

God never does the unnecessary. He gives sight to the blind, not to those who can already see. He heals the sick, not those who are healthy. He lifts up the fallen, not those who are still standing. And, in this same way, He raises up the "nobodies" of this world, not those who are already "somebodies."

When Jesus was on the earth, He went to the needy. And God still meets us at the point of our need, not at the point of our preferences. This is because need produces desire.

David had an all-consuming desire for God, and it was that desire that elevated him to the throne of Israel. God knew that David wasn't after position or power. His all-consuming desire was not to be wealthy, to have a crown on his head, or to hear people calling him "King." No, David would have been satisfied to be a doorkeeper in God's house. He said:

> *For a day in Your courts is better than a thousand. I would rather be a doorkeeper in the house of my God than dwell in the tents of wickedness. For the Lord God is a sun and shield; The Lord will give grace and glory; No good thing will He withhold from those who walk uprightly. O Lord of hosts, blessed is the man who trusts in You!*
>
> Psalm 84:10-12

David was intent on seeking after God, and what we seek is what we get. If what you desire is illicit drugs, then you'll become a drug addict. If you desire alcohol, you'll become an alcoholic. If your desire is a perverted sexual lust, then you'll eventually have a perverted, lusting demon in you.

What is your greatest desire? Some would actually say a better golf game, to star in the NBA, or to become the CEO of a large company. What is it that you think about when you go to bed at night? What fills your thoughts each new day? Well, whatever it is, that's what you'll become, for your desire ultimately determines your destiny.

As Solomon was being anointed to take his father's place as king over Israel, God asked him a loaded question:

> *In Gibeon the Lord appeared to Solomon in a dream by night: and God said, Ask what I shall give thee.*
>
> 1 Kings 3:5

This was Solomon's opportunity. God was handing him a blank check. So what would he ask God for? Riches? Fame? Beautiful women?

Those who pray without desire are praying vain, repetitious, and empty prayers...

ꙮ

Solomon's choice that day showed where his heart was. He asked God for wisdom to rule well. Because of that, God said that he would not only have wisdom, but also all of the things he had not asked for. Thus Solomon became the wisest man of his time and also one of the richest.

Those who pray without desire are praying vain, repetitious, and empty prayers, and I'm afraid that God doesn't even hear them. They've lost their *"first love,"* and they need to return to God's altar and get new fire in their souls.

THE DESIRE OF FIRST LOVE

When people first get saved, they experience what the Bible calls their *"first love"*:

I have somewhat against thee, because thou hast left thy first love.

Revelation 2:4

I am convinced that our *"first love"* represents God's perfect will for our lives. He places certain desires in us, and we hunger for those specific things. This changes everything about our lives.

"First love" is contagious. You're excited, and you want to tell everyone about it. You want to go to church every time the

doors are open. You just can't get enough of the Word of God. On your lunch hour, you sit and read the Bible or some good Christian book. Your appetite for God seems endless.

You don't just go to church on Sundays; you can hardly wait for Wednesday night to come (or whatever night your church has a mid-week service). I have people call me to ask, "Do you know anyone who's having church on Mondays? Wednesday is too long for me to wait." That's what first love will do for you. It puts within you a seemingly inexhaustible desire for more of God.

"First love" also gives you a desire to work for God. After I got saved, all I wanted to do was preach. Every time I saw someone preaching, I thought, "I want to preach just like that, if God would just give me sermons to deliver." I was so serious about this that I actually began outlining sermons that I hoped to someday deliver.

As it turned out, I wasn't able to go into ministry right away because Lawrence and I got married and had children, and it took all of my efforts to raise them. For a while, it seemed that my dream of preaching would never come true, but God hadn't forgotten it—and I hadn't forgotten it either.

The reason I eventually did begin preaching after such a long delay was that the desire to preach had never left me. God puts a desire in your heart, as part of your first love. In that moment, your desire and His desire become one, and that union of desire will eventually bring forth the intended fruit—if you determine never to lose your *"first love."* As we will see in the next chapter, you actually become pregnant with desire, and nothing can satisfy you until you've given birth to that desire.

Spiritual Desire

THE DANGER OF SETTLING IN

Most of us are excited and enthusiastic in the blush of our *"first love,"* but after a while, we seem to cool off, and then we sit back and start to live more "normally." As we saw in the last chapter, that seems to be what happened to the man at the Pool of Bethesda. When he had first come there, he no doubt had the thrill of hope. But when he saw others being healed, and he wasn't healed, he became disillusioned. No one wanted to help him, no one wanted to open doors for him, and no one seemed to give him a chance. Instead, they pushed ahead of him and got their portion, and he was left in despair.

Sometimes, in the church, not only does it seem like no one wants to help us get ahead; some actually seem to be trying to push us down or push us aside. That doesn't feel very good, and it can quickly result in our desire turning to disappointment. I'm afraid that what we have in a great many churches is a group of disillusioned and cool people.

In far too many churches, a fired-up choir/and or worship leader is trying to stir a group of people to worship, and it's like pulling teeth. Did you ever try to lead a group of dead people in worship? It's no fun at all.

This is what the Scriptures mean when they say:

This know also, that in the last days perilous times shall come. For men shall be lovers of their own selves, covetous, boasters, proud, blasphemers, disobedient to parents, unthankful, unholy, without natural affection, trucebreakers, false accusers, incontinent, fierce, despisers of those that are good, traitors, heady, highminded, lovers of pleasures more than lovers of God; HAVING A

FORM OF GODLINESS, BUT DENYING THE POWER THEREOF: from such turn away.

2 Timothy 3:1-5

I'm afraid that this describes many churches. They're going through the motions, doing all the right things, saying all the right words, singing the right tunes, but all of this holy activity doesn't seem to be going anywhere.

Whatever you do, don't lose hope that things will get better. Desire changed the life of blind Bartimaeus, the life of the woman of Canaan and that of her daughter, and the life of the crippled man at the Pool of Bethesda. It will change your life too.

Desire brings forth destiny because when you have an insatiable desire for God, nothing can discourage you. People can do what they will, and you will keep pressing forward. You will refuse to live your life in pouting and pity, and nothing will keep you from God and His house.

People might say unkind things about you, and it will hurt. But your desire for God will cause you to overlook it and go on.

Desire will cause you to be the first one at the altar and the last one to leave the church building. In this way, your desire will determine your destiny in life.

SATAN'S UNHOLY DESIRE

Whatever your godly desire happens to be, you can be sure that Satan is intent upon causing you to forget it and lay it aside. He has his own ideas about your destiny, and you must refuse to do as he urges.

Satan knows that your desire is God-given, and it will work to destroy his kingdom, so he will do anything he can to discourage you. Stand fast against him.

Just as God has a holy desire for each of us, Satan has an evil desire for each of us. He desired to do Peter damage because he knew how much good Peter could do for the kingdom of God.

The original language of that passage gives the sense that Satan demanded permission to have Peter, but God refused. Let's look more closely at the passage:

And the Lord said, Simon, Simon, behold, Satan hath desired to have you, that he may sift you as wheat: but I have prayed for thee, that thy faith fail not: and when thou art converted, strengthen thy brethren.

Luke 22:31-32

This phrase *"when thou art converted,"* in the original Greek, conveys the meaning, "when you retrace your steps." It was only after Peter had retraced his steps that he would be personally convinced of the truth, and only then could he strengthen his brothers. At the moment this was spoken, he wasn't sure, but after Jesus had died and then resurrected, he would retrace his steps, see that everything Jesus had said was true, and that He was the Son of God. Then he would be ready to convert others.

It's time that each of us retrace our steps. Go back and take another look, and in the process, let spiritual desire be rekindled.

Didn't God heal you once or more than once? Didn't He miraculously supply your needs on several occasions or even many occasions? Didn't He bring you out of trouble? Well, if He did that once, can He not do it again? After all, He's *"the same yesterday, and to day and for ever"* (Hebrews 13:8). He said:

For I am the Lord, I change not.

Malachi 3:6

Just as He did for Peter, God will stand in the gap and make up the hedge for you. He will fight to see that you keep your desire. But it's up to you to see that you continue to seek Him. You should because He's never failed you yet. It is as you persevere in Him that your desire will bring forth your destiny.

TWO RAMPANT SINS IN THE CHURCH

I am sad to say that there are two sins that seem to be out of control in the church, and they are robbing many of their destiny. For some reason, these two sins seem very difficult for modern Christians to resist. They are pride and sexual immorality. If Satan can't get people with one of these, he tries the other one.

Pride says, "I deserve it," and sexual immorality says, "I need it," and the two of them work together. This gives us a clue as to how Satan works. He will say to a good Christian man, "It's not right the way your wife's treating you. You deserve better than that. She gives you such a hard time that you would be justified to cheat on her. Nobody could blame you if you did, because they surely couldn't live under what you live under."

Amazingly, these lies seem to work, and amazingly, the combination of these two temptations overcomes many. It then becomes difficult for the people involved to overcome the resulting reproach. Their destiny is either delayed or totally destroyed.

In truth, pride appeals to empty heads, and sexual enticement appeals to empty hearts. But try to tell someone that when they are caught in the jaws of temptation. When these unhealthy desires are activated, people absolutely refuse to take advice. All they want is satisfaction.

In truth, pride appeals to empty heads, and sexual enticement appeals to empty hearts.

Since this onslaught has affected so many in the body of Christ, we must each prepare ourselves for an attack of the enemy. My feeling is that the way we can prepare for such a temptation is by deciding ahead of time how we want to react when it inevitably comes. Resistance is easier if the decision to resist has been made.

Temptation will come. I'm sixty now, and men still flirt with me. When it happens, I let them know right away who I am and what I do, and that usually stops it.

"God bless you," I say. "I'm a preacher. What do you do?" That seems to cool things off very quickly.

Recently I was traveling with another of our ladies, and the man who helped me with my suitcase in the airport began to flirt with me. "Boy, you look nice," he began.

"Well, thank you," I said (meaning to thank him for helping me with the suitcase), and then I turned to walk away.

"I love your shoes," he said, and I realized that he hadn't gotten the message.

"Thanks again," I answered. "See you!" And I never looked back. I was not about to let that man rob me of my destiny.

BE PREPARED FOR TEMPTATION

The Bible admonishes us:

A prudent man foreseeth the evil, and hideth himself: but the simple pass on, and are punished.

Proverbs 22:3

Prudent people prepare for danger, but the simple just plunge on into it and have to suffer the consequences. One prudent step to be taken before reaching for the forbidden fruit might be to take a long and hard look at what has happened to those who have given in to such temptation.

I don't understand it completely, but there's something hypnotic and intoxicating about wickedness. One thing leads to another, and at some point, there seems to be a total disregard for consequences. David said:

The desire of the wicked shall perish.

Psalm 112:10

Too many times, our appetites become our masters, and we become willing to do anything at all to satisfy them. And what is an appetite if not a desire?

Always, when our appetites are for the things of God, Satan comes along with his lies and deceptions and tries to turn us away to other things. If we know the truth in God, we can easily turn him away.

"No, Satan," we can respond. "There was a time when I was tempted by drugs, but no longer. Now I know a satisfaction and excitement that nothing can surpass." Or we can say to him, "No, Satan. There was a time when I was tempted by a good-looking man, but no more. Now I know a Man who truly understands me and stands by me whatever may come. Since He's been so good to me, I can't afford to let Him down for some momentary thrill." My destiny is too important to let it be damaged or destroyed.

EVEN JESUS WAS TEMPTED

Satan was foolish enough to think that he could deceive even Jesus himself. He took the Lord up to a high place and said to Him:

If thou be the Son of God, cast thyself down: for it is written, He shall give his angels charge concerning thee: and in their hands they shall bear thee up, lest at any time thou dash thy foot against a stone.

Matthew 4:6

Jesus wasn't about to fall for that line. He answered without hesitation:

It is written again, Thou shalt not tempt the Lord thy God.

Matthew 4:7

In other words, Jesus was saying, "You can't fool Me!"

This was devastating for Satan because he had taken his best shot at Jesus. After one more attempt to subvert the Lord of Lords, he took his leave and ran with his tail between his legs.

That's not to say that Satan gave up trying to destroy Jesus. Later, when Jesus had read the Scriptures in the synagogue in His home town, Satan inspired the crowd to rush Him and try to push Him off a nearby cliff. In the process, Jesus disappeared out of their sight.

So let the devil push. If you stay true to God, the evil one can't do you any harm. God has promised to hide you under the shadow of His wings:

He that dwelleth in the secret place of the most High shall abide under the shadow of the Almighty.

Psalm 91:1

God has placed eternity in our hearts, so it should not surprise us that earthly things fail to satisfy us. And just as long as eternity is in our hearts, we can stand in the face of temptation and laugh at the enemy.

You can say to Satan, "Take this whole world, but give me Jesus. I'm never turning back. My destiny is too important to allow you to steal it."

God is doing all that He can to help us stand strong in this day, and one of the things He has done is to flood us with His Word. We need it because we just don't have time to "mess up."

Because God has given us so much of His Word, we have no excuse. Just say no to temptation, and the more you resist, the stronger you'll become.

It's a lot like a good workout with weight-training devices. The greater the resistance, the stronger you become. And the stronger you become, the more likely you are to find your true destiny in God.

IT'S TIME TO GET EXCITED ABOUT GOD

When you get more excited about prayer than you do about going out on Friday night, things will change in your life. When you get more excited about being with God than about being with your other loved ones, then things will change in your life. When you get more excited about spending Monday night at church in prayer than spending it watching Monday Night Football, then things will change in your life.

When you get hungry enough for God, you'll sometimes lose all desire to eat. "I'm going to fast for the next few days," you'll tell your spouse and children, and your desire will bring you to a whole new level in God.

Are you delighting yourself in the Lord? Are you delighted to go to His house? Are you delighted to read His Word? Are you delighted to spend time with Him in prayer? If not, let God re-ignite your passion for Him and give you a flaming desire to have more of His love and power.

You may have wondered why something you have wanted badly from God has not yet come. Have you shown Him that you want it more than anything else? He may be waiting to see how serious you are, how badly you really want it.

Another reason may be that when something costs you a great deal, you value it more, and you don't let go of it easily. Many of us will never backslide because we've paid a great price to be where we are today.

LET GOD RESTORE YOUR FIRE

What is your desire today? Have you let those desires of *"first love"* die within you? Have you aborted the dream before it had a chance to come to life? Have you had a spiritual miscarriage? The Bible has encouraging news:

The gifts and calling of God are without repentance.

Romans 11:29

God hasn't changed His mind about you, and His gifts are still available to you. Like the daughter of Jairus, they may be sleeping, but they can easily and quickly come to life again.

Just speak to that gift, and let it be reborn. Let God restore to you a desire for Him and the things of His kingdom, a desire to bring others to His feet, a desire to witness, a desire to be all that God has intended you to be.

If you need to, get to an altar of prayer. If you can't do that, make an altar there where you are. Say, "Father, rekindle my desire because I'm not where I want to be. I want to go somewhere in You and do something great for You. Help me."

Maybe your desire has totally died. You still go to church, but only out of obligation. There's no hunger in you for the things of God. You have no desire to attend prayer meetings. You no longer have a place where you get alone with God and just bask in His presence. When you walk outside in your yard or around the neighborhood, you no longer marvel at His glory and let His great creation inspire you to worship. Let God turn that around for you.

Your desire may be taking you down the road to destruction. Have you begun to desire the things of this world? Do you long to go back to what used to excite you: drugs, alcohol, or some sexual perversion? You can't afford to go that route.

If the fire has grown cold in you, come back to God. Tell Him, "I desire You, Lord, more than anything. I give You all my hopes and dreams. Have Your way in my life today." He will not disappoint you. He will rekindle your love for Him and set your soul on fire afresh and anew. Don't delay another day, for your desire will determine your destiny. There is an inseparable link between the two.

Chapter 3

GIVING BIRTH TO YOUR DESIRE

A voice of noise from the city, a voice from the temple, a voice of the Lord that rendereth recompense to his enemies. Before she travailed, she brought forth; before her pain came, she was delivered of a man child. Who hath heard such a thing? who hath seen such things? Shall the earth be made to bring forth in one day? or shall a nation be born at once? for as soon as Zion travailed, she brought forth her children.

Isaiah 66:6-8

God has a desire for your life, and, as we have seen, when His desire becomes your desire, a unity of desire is formed that is not easily broken. You have formed a holy union with the God

41

of the universe and, in the process, you've actually become pregnant with His desire. That changes everything.

If you've ever experienced pregnancy, you know exactly what I'm talking about. Everything you do now revolves around the fact that you have a life growing inside of you. You can't go the same places and do the same things as before. You can't even eat the same things. Life is no longer about you; it's about the life growing inside of you.

Personally, my life is no longer about satisfying the whims of Darlene Bishop; it's about the gift and calling of God that's upon me. Because of that, I can't live like the average person does or do the things they do. And I don't want to. I have a special gift from God, a special calling, and with that special calling comes a special responsibility. I have something to deliver to God's people, and I must deliver it.

THE CHANGES PREGNANCY BRINGS

When any woman becomes pregnant in the natural, her whole life changes. With every decision she makes, she must now take into consideration the fact that she's pregnant. She goes to bed thinking about it and wakes up the next day thinking about it. Because of this, she does everything necessary to protect that life and to prepare to bring it forth.

It's the same when you become pregnant with godly desire. Every time you go to church, you feel something leap within you. And there are many things you will no longer consider doing.

Every time an old boyfriend calls you and says, "Can we get together tonight?" you'll answer, "I can't. I'm pregnant."

Every time someone offers you a drink from the bar, you'll answer, "No, thank you. I'm pregnant." Every time Sister Doolittle approaches you and says, "Have you heard about Brother Doless?" you'll answer, "I can't listen to this because I'm pregnant." Lots of things change in your life when you become pregnant with God's desires, and you don't resent the changes. You're excited about the new life inside of you and willing to make whatever sacrifice is necessary to protect it.

When you're pregnant, you'll become a dedicated follower of Jesus. No one will have to do a follow-up program with you. The church won't have to send a committee to your door to entice you to come to their services. When you're pregnant, you'll come early and leave late because you don't know when the baby might come.

After you have become pregnant with desire, you put yourself on guard at all times against danger that might affect the life you're carrying. You guard, or keep, your heart with all diligence because you know that's where Satan will try to come in. As the wisdom of the Proverbs declares:

Keep thy heart with all diligence; for out of it are the issues of life.

Proverbs 4:23

Remembering how Satan was able to enter Judas, one of the twelve chosen disciples of Jesus, and what the dreadful result was, you'll be careful to guard your own life. This word *keep,* as used in Proverbs 4:23, is a military term that signifies a guard standing at a door preventing anyone from going into it. That's exactly what you do when you're pregnant.

MISCARRIAGES DO HAPPEN

But miscarriages do happen, and with the first sign of a miscarriage, you know that you have lost your desire. Miscarriage simply means to miss what you were carrying. Suddenly, there's no more life in you. You go to church, but the worship no longer sounds the same. You don't enjoy the fellowship of other believers as much.

Suddenly that old boyfriend begins to look good to you again. Now you'll accept something from the bar because no one will know if it's an alcoholic drink or just a juice. Lots of things change when you've miscarried. It is not a happy time, and it often leaves you disoriented and reeling with confusion.

But I have good news. If you have miscarried and the seed of godly desire no longer burns within your soul, God wants to plant a new seed in your womb. Let Him impregnate you with desire afresh today. Let the desire that died inside of you leap back to life. He can do that so easily and quickly.

The desire God now plants in you may be to become a Sunday school teacher. It may be a desire to prophesy or to lay hands on the sick and see them recover. Get ready for your particular God-inspired desire to spring to life in your innermost being. When you are willing to carry His life, God honors your desire.

YOUR NEW FOCUS

When you have a burning God-inspired desire, it becomes the focal point of every prayer meeting. Every time you meet with God, you can hardly wait to get around to asking Him about it. You pray for other things, for the preacher and his or her family, for the nations and for the people of Israel. But, all the while, you're chomping at the bit to talk to God about the seed He has planted within you.

You come to recognize that whenever you're able to pray about your desire, a strange satisfaction comes over you. It seems that the more you pray about it, the more pregnant you become. And the more pregnant you become, the sooner you can hold that baby in your arms. Prayer is the midwife that will help to bring it forth.

> *Many have aborted the plan that God has for them because they've been unwilling to pay the price in prayer.*

Many have aborted the plan that God has for them because they've been unwilling to pay the price in prayer. Many women get abortions these days for no other reason than the fact that they're selfish. They're not ready to give themselves over to such great responsibility.

Many think they want to be in Christian ministry ... until they discover that Christian ministry requires a whole lot more than just holding a microphone in your hand. In fact, it requires a complete surrender of every aspect of your life to God.

TRAVAILING IN PRAYER

Your ministry will come forth only through much travail, and many people don't like that fact. In the Word of God, travail is always connected with grief, pain, and sorrow, and that's no fun. And yet birth doesn't happen without travail.

I remember vividly the details of the birth of my youngest daughter, Julie. When I got to the hospital, I was given a shot of something that was intended to relax me. In reality, it sedated me.

"This will relax you, Mrs. Bishop," a nurse said. The next thing I knew someone was slapping my face, trying to get me awake. They were saying, "Wake up, Mrs. Bishop, wake up. Your baby's ready to be born, and you've got to bear down and push. If you don't bear down and push, this baby's life will be in jeopardy."

BEARING DOWN

Travail requires a bearing down and a pushing forth, but I was still so sedated that it was hard for me to respond. I heard what they were saying to me, and it registered in my consciousness that my baby's life was in jeopardy, but I couldn't seem to muster the strength to do anything about it.

I would make a noise and grunt like I was pushing, but I wasn't awake enough to really push. It was all lip service. I was like those who have *"a form of godliness, but deny the power thereof"* (2 Timothy 3:5). Like the hypocrites Jesus spoke of, I might have been confessing it with my mouth, but my heart was far from it (see Matthew 15:8). I was going through the motions, but nothing was happening.

They tried slapping me several more times, to get me to cooperate with them, but still they had to use forceps to bring Julie out. When I saw her the next day, there were visible marks on her head where they had pulled her from me. I had been so sedated that I wasn't able to help push as much as I should have.

Somehow I think that the church of today has been sedated. "How is that?" some might ask. We've been sedated by teachings that say we no longer have to pray through a given situation. We can just confess it, speaking the Word, naming and claiming what we want, and it's ours. But I've got news for all those who think that the Christian life is that easy. Anything and everything you get from God will come by you praying a hole through heaven to get it.

This is serious because our churches are full of people who have no idea how to pray. No idea!

TRAVAIL BRINGS FORTH LIFE

One week in 1999, I called on as many of the people of our church as would to fast with me for three days, from Thursday through Saturday. Then I asked them to meet me at the church on Saturday morning for a special service of travail. "We're going to travail until we birth something in the Spirit," I told them.

I was serious. Travail in the Spirit may be a term that is nearly foreign to most modern American believers, but I'm convinced that it will have to be called back into the church if we're to see the result God has destined for us. Sadly, what we have today is an imitation of the real travail, and most people don't know the difference. We come to church and are entertained and leave feeling pretty good about ourselves, but because there's no anointing to break the yokes of bondage off of us, some people leave the church building the same as when they came in. It's time for us to get serious about travail and bring to birth our destiny.

That Saturday I was in the children's church area of our building, lying on the floor behind the soundboard, when I felt the spirit of travail come over me. I suddenly felt a great burden for my oldest brother Dale, and I began to weep and call out to God for his soul.

Dale was fifty-six years old about then, but he still weighed only a hundred and five pounds. He contracted polio shortly after he was born, and, as a result, his body never developed fully. When he eventually began to walk, it was with a very bad limp.

Because of Dale's physical limitations, children made fun of him in school, and this led him to develop a very bad attitude toward life. One night he was in a bar, trying to drown his sorrows, trying to forget for a moment his bitterness and anger. Another man who was drinking in the bar came after him, and Dale shot and killed him. He spent several years in prison for that incident, and when he came out, he was more bitter and hard-hearted than ever.

While he was in prison, Dale promised me that he would get saved once he was released. But when that day came, he felt that he had lost a lot of time and had a lot of living to catch up on. So he went right back to his former life.

Dale was angry at the whole world. He got mad at his son one night and shot him in the leg. He also wanted to kill my youngest brother.

The sad thing is that we came from a good family. Our parents were good people, but the devil doesn't care whose life he trashes. He'll invade your house, if he can get away with it. I've walked through more prison gates and spent time in more courtrooms than I ever imagined I would. But that Saturday morning I sensed that something was changing with Dale.

I had fallen on my face before God, and as the travail came, I said to Him, "I will not get up from this place until I feel a change in Dale's life."

That was saying a lot. Dale was now insisting that there was no God and that he hated everyone in our family. He hadn't spoken a word to our mother in five years. "I'm believing for his salvation!" I cried out, and I stayed there in travail for his soul until I felt a release come.

BIRTH AT LAST

Three days later Dale had an accident on a four-wheeler. He was airlifted to a hospital in Nashville, Tennessee, and someone called to say that they didn't know if he would live or die. "Oh God," I prayed, "surely, surely this is his opportunity to know You."

I knew what I had felt in the Spirit that Saturday morning, and I was sure that Dale's salvation was as good as accomplished. No one could tell me any different.

It is no secret that the concept of praying people through to salvation in this way is a very old-fashioned one, one that most modern Christians have never even heard of. But that doesn't make it any less effective. If you're in the kingdom of God today, it's because someone prayed for you. And we need much more of this deep spiritual prayer today.

We often get people to come forward in an altar call, but then we have to wonder what has happened to them. The following week we can't find them. Are they to blame? Or is this a weakness of the church at large? Not nearly enough prayer is going up these days for new creatures in the kingdom.

As I made my way to the hospital to see Dale, I was sure that a great change had already come to his life. I was surprised to find him "cussing out" his doctors and nurses.

"I told that one over there that if I'd had a shotgun, I'd have blown her brains out," he said, and I cringed. What was happening? I knew what I'd felt. I had wept that day until there were no more tears to weep, and I had pushed and borne down until I had no more strength. With great pain, I had howled and lamented and wailed before God, because I could see Dale being shaken over hell, and I knew that I was his lifeline. I had been determined not to give up until Dale was safely inside the Kingdom, and I was sure that God had answered my prayer.

All of that had been so real, and yet now there didn't seem to be any change at all. I would just have to trust God and wait to see the fruit of my faith. I went back home and committed it all to God.

About a week later, early one morning, I received a phone call. It was Dale. "Sis," he said, "I just got saved about four o'clock this morning. How can I reach Mamma and Daddy? I've got some things I need to make right with them."

I said, "Baby, I already knew it. Three weeks ago, I saw it all, as I was on my face before God in prayer for you." Oh, how we rejoiced together!

That's just how powerful it is to travail in God, and it will always bring your desire to birth.

SHOULD OTHERS DO OUR PRAYING?

Today we're so lazy and preoccupied with other things that we ask others to do our praying for us. An evangelist friend of mine told me about what happened in one of his recent meet-ings. A woman came up to him and asked him if he would pray for her husband to be saved. Something came over him, and he answered her in this way: "Sister, have you ever prayed all night long for your husband to be saved?"

"No," she admitted, "I don't suppose I have."

"Have you ever prayed for one solid hour for nothing but the salvation of your husband?" he continued.

She thought for a moment and then answered, "Well, I don't suppose I have prayed for him for a solid hour without stopping."

The evangelist then told her, "Why would you ask me to pray for a man I've never met, when he's your husband, and you haven't even prayed for him for one hour? Go sit down."

The woman was highly offended and swore that she would never return to that church as long as the man was there. She thought he was about the meanest man she'd ever met, and she would show him.

Her husband was out of town on a business trip (some two hundred miles away), and when she returned home, she decided that she would pray just for him for a whole hour. With that, she got serious with God, and before long, a spirit of travail came upon her, and she began lamenting and crying out to God.

About three o'clock that next morning, her husband was suddenly awakened with a desire to call his wife. When he couldn't get an answer, he became alarmed. Something must be terribly wrong.

He jumped in his car and drove for four hours until he reached their home. At seven o'clock in the morning, he was pulling into the driveway. He jumped out, rushed to get the door open and get inside and into their bedroom. There he found his wife lying on her face, groaning with pain.

He grabbed her up in his arms and fired off several things in short order: "What's the matter with you? I drove all night! Why didn't you answer my call early this morning?"

...many of us seem to know how to organize, but we no longer know how to agonize.

Her answer startled him: "Because I've been praying for you since eleven o'clock last night."

He fell on his knees right there and got saved. The next night, she took him with her to the revival meetings.

"This is what I got for praying all night long!" she proudly declared to the evangelist and everyone else present." That's the power of travailing prayer, and it's because you are giving birth to godly desire.

CAN WE NOW ORGANIZE BUT NO LONGER AGONIZE?

Many Christian women have thought that they wanted their husbands saved, but that's about all they've done about it—think. They haven't bothered to take the necessary time and make the necessary effort to pray their loved one through to salvation.

In the church world today, many of us seem to know how to organize, but we no longer know how to agonize. Most of us don't know anything about praying until we're sure that an answer is on its way.

Saying a little prayer is not enough. You have to go to God with true desire and pray out of that desire until your God-inspired petition is fulfilled.

But how can you know when it's time to give birth to your desire? Oh, that's easy. When the pain is more than you can bear, you'll know that it's time. When one of your children is so "messed up" that you don't know what to do next, when you no longer have any answers to life's many problems, when your husband has gone on a rampage and nothing seems to reach him … that's when you'll know that you're ready to give birth.

When it happens, the pain will intensify, and one pain will no more than pass than another will be upon you. At this point, you'll know that your desire is about to come forth. When trial follows trial and dilemma follows dilemma, don't despair. Rather, get ready to give birth to something new and wonderful.

Desperation is a wonderful aid to prayer. It makes you get deadly serious before God and helps you give birth to your desire.

NEEDED: MOTHERS IN ISRAEL

Deborah, of Old Testament fame, knew what it was to become desperate before God, and because of that, she became *"a mother in Israel"*:

> *In the days of Shamgar the son of Anath, in the days of Jael, the highways were unoccupied, and the travellers walked through byways. The inhabitants of the villages ceased, they ceased in Israel, until that I Deborah arose, that I arose a MOTHER IN ISRAEL.*
>
> Judges 5:6-7

Deborah had a desire, but a desire was not enough. She had to get desperate enough to do something about the current situation. And she did just that. Oh, how we need more mothers in Israel in the church today!

Mothers are more than women who can give birth to a baby. Mothers know how to care for a baby and raise it properly. Where are all of our mothers in Israel? I'm afraid that they're busy at the spa, the cinema, or the mall.

A real mother knows how to pray because she's discerning. She senses it when her baby's in trouble. She looks for the presence of drugs because she knows that something's causing him to act differently.

Real mothers should be teaching our current generation how to raise children themselves. Paul wrote:

The aged women likewise, that they be in behaviour as becometh holiness, not false accusers, not given to much wine, teachers of good things; that they may teach the young women to be sober, to love their husbands, to love their children, to be discreet, chaste, keepers at home, good, obedient to their own husbands, that the word of God be not blasphemed.

Titus 2:3-5

We're still teaching the younger women, but we're only teaching them things like how to fix their hair, how to dress properly, and how to use makeup. It's time that we taught them how to effectively call on Jesus, how to plead His blood over themselves and their family, and how to pray through until victory comes.

It's time that we commit to a new generation the standards that have brought us strength down through the centuries. There was a time here in America when the church set the standards, and the whole country lived by them. Now, it seems, the world sets the standards, and the church lives by them. This ought not to be!

DESIRE ALWAYS BRINGS FORTH FRUIT

My daddy always planted a garden, and I couldn't help but notice that when he planted squash, its vines took off in all directions. They would pass through the corn, the beans, the potato patch, and the tomato plants, and in time, they would be intertwined with absolutely everything in the garden. Still, the squash plants never changed their nature. Although they were intertwined with everything else, they were still squash, and they still brought forth squash.

This is what I've found to be true also of people who are pregnant with desire. You can place them in a factory, standing alongside a person who's demon possessed, and they can eat their lunch with an atheist, and have a boss who's some kind of pervert, and still they'll never change. Despite the fact that they're forced to listen to every imaginable cursing and perversion all day long, when they walk out of that factory door to go home, they're still a child of God, and they're still pregnant with His desires.

One summer I was preaching in a conference in Canada, and one day I went into a nail salon there to get my nails done. There was a nice-looking young man there, a hair dresser, and he came over to where I was getting my nails done and began to talk to me.

"Are you from this area?" he asked.

"No, sir," I said, "I'm from Ohio."

"So what are you doing here in town?" he asked.

I said, "I'm speaking at a local conference."

"Well," he mused, "how long will you be here?"

"Just four days," I told him.

"Well, what are you doing tonight?" he asked brazenly.

"I'm preaching tonight," I said.

"Okay," he answered, "but after you get done, would you like to go out for caviar?"

"Oh, I don't think my husband would appreciate that," I said, laughing.

"Is he here with you?" he asked.

"No," I said.

"Well, then, what's the problem?" he asked.

I said, "The problem is that I'm preaching. Why don't you come tonight and hear me preach?"

"I will," he said. And then he added, "If you'll go out with me afterward."

I had a young lady with me that day, and she was furious with his brazenness. Later, she said to me, "Oh, I got so angry with that young man! I was rebuking the devil! How brazen of the devil to try to tempt you like that. I was praying for you the whole time."

I smiled. "That was no temptation," I assured her. "I'm pregnant! The last thing I need is a boyfriend or a one-night stand."

Once you have brought your desire to birth, it's yours, and no one can take it from you. As I noted in an earlier chapter, Paul wrote: *"The gifts and calling of God are without repentance"* (Romans 11:29). Yours is an irrevocable privilege and responsibility. You might, at some point, neglect this new life, and you might even forsake it, but it will still belong to you. When you get into God's presence, you will feel His nudgings and know that you can still bring forth your dream—whatever men may say.

THE INABILITY TO CONCEIVE

In order to become pregnant, you first have to be able to conceive. The reason some can't conceive is that they're convinced that God can never use them. After all, they don't have much education. Surely, nobody would listen to them. They're just not the type. So they remain barren.

But I beg to differ. I dropped out of school in the eleventh grade, and Lawrence and I got married. Fifteen months later, I had a baby girl, and about two years after that I had another baby, a boy this time. Six years after that, I had another girl, and four years after that I had a third baby girl.

But all of that time, I was pregnant with something else. At the age of fourteen, when I got saved, I experienced God implanting a seed in my womb, as I mentioned earlier in the book, the desire to preach. It didn't start to come to fulfillment until I was thirty-eight years old. Still, at that point, I hadn't had any further education (not a single day of seminary), and all I'd done was be a mama to my four children. Still, at that age, I stood and preached my first sermon. I was glad that day for Jeremiah's words:

Thus saith the Lord, Let not the wise man glory in his wisdom, neither let the mighty man glory in his might, let not the rich man glory in his riches: but let him that glorieth glory in this, that he understandeth and knoweth me, that I am the Lord which exercise lovingkindness, judgment, and righteousness, in the earth: for in these things I delight, saith the Lord.

Jeremiah 9:23-24

It is only knowing God that qualifies us to be impregnated with His desire and then to carry it to term.

GET READY

Get ready to give birth to your desire. You've been through enough pain. Now it's time to bring your dream to reality.

If you're serious with God, get on your face before Him in prayer.

If your son is away at war, let the spirit of travail take hold of you for him. Let the labor pains intensify. Give way to the lamentation and howling that is rising up from your soul today. I guarantee you that things will not be the same again in your life or his.

If you're serious with God, get on your face before Him in prayer. Cry out for that child, for that gift to be manifested in your life. Wail and lament. Pray a hole right through hell and take back what the devil has stolen from you.

If you have a suitable prayer partner, agree together in travail. Labor together. Bear down and push your way through to victory. Refuse to allow hell to have what is yours.

We've been lying around on ivory couches too long. It's time to bring forth life, and your work won't be finished until you have delivered it.

Cry out! Let the hot tears flow! If you don't know what to say, then just groan! Do as Joel so aptly described:

> *Let the priests, the ministers of the Lord, weep between the porch and the altar, and let them say, Spare thy people, O Lord, and give not thine heritage to reproach, that the heathen should rule over them: wherefore should they say among the people, Where is their God?*
>
> Joel 2:17

Why are our children not saved? We haven't had enough desire for them to be saved. We have insisted on three square meals a day, and that has made our bodies very round, but we need to fast more. Desire demands it.

Do whatever you have to do. Refuse to give up. Lift up your voice like a trumpet. Let the devil know that you mean business. This is not a prayer about "the sweet by and by." You have to storm the gates of hell and take back what has been stolen.

Jesus said *"the violent"* would take the kingdom *"by force"*:

> *And from the days of John the Baptist until now the kingdom of heaven suffereth violence, and the violent take it by force.*
>
> Matthew 11:12

Get serious. You wouldn't allow another person to beat up on your baby, and yet you've stood by and watched as the devil stomped your children into the ground. It's time to say, "No more!" Let him know that you're taking back what is rightfully yours.

This is the kind of prayer that the church mothers were accustomed to praying in the past, the kind of prayer your grandmother prayed for you. When nothing else would do, she howled and lamented before God. And that's why you're in the kingdom today. Now it's your turn to pray for others until they are birthed into the kingdom.

Don't give up until you feel the labor pains subside. You're on the right track. The psalmist declared:

Weeping may endure for a night, but joy cometh in the morning.

Psalm 30:5

Don't stop praying until you feel that spirit of joy coming upon you. It may come as laughter. Then you'll know that the baby has come forth in the name of Jesus.

WHAT ARE YOU BIRTHING?

What are you birthing? You are giving birth to your God-inspired desire.

Some of you may need to give birth to your healing. You've been sick much too long. When that baby comes forth, you'll find not only that you're personally healed, but also that you can now lay hands on other sick people and see them healed. You're not just carrying a desire for personal healing; your spiritual pregnancy will bring forth a gift of healing.

Some of you will become prophets and prophetesses through travail. For a long time now, you've been carrying a desire to prophesy. That desire is from God. Bring it forth.

Some of you carry a desire to teach or a desire to preach. Those thoughts are not your own. They're God's desires implanted within your spirit. Now God wants to bring that gift forth, so don't give up until you feel it happen.

Lift your voice as loud as you can, and begin to pray in the Holy Ghost. When you do that, your prayers go straight to the throne of God. This makes sure the devil is powerless to block them.

He has told you that you'll never get what you're believing for, but he's a liar. God is about to do something in you that He's never done before. When we wait upon God, answers come. Your destiny comes to life.

IT'S TIME TO CELEBRATE

Once the travail has ended and the desire has come forth, it's time to celebrate. It's time to give God the praise due to His name. Get excited, and let the world know that you've been delivered. You have something to shout about, so take your liberty. God has been good to you, so let Him know that you appreciate it.

He is a celebrating God, and you can be sure that all of heaven is celebrating with you. You have given birth to your desire, and there is an inseparable link between your desire and your destiny.

Chapter 4

THE SIN OF PRAYERLESSNESS

As for me, God forbid that I should sin against the Lord in ceasing to pray for you.

1 Samuel 12:23

I firmly believe that prayerlessness is one of the greatest sins of the American church today. It's a sin against man, just as much as it's a sin against God, and we're all guilty of this sin to some degree. We've all fallen short in this area.

But some have fallen so far short in regard to prayer that their spiritual lives are endangered. Or is it just the opposite? Has their spiritual lukewarmness caused them to become lazy about prayer? Whatever the case, prayerlessness has caused many to turn back from serving God and to serve their own flesh. It's time that we recognize the seriousness of this sin and do something about it.

WHAT IS PRAYER AND WHY IS IT SO IMPORTANT?

What exactly is prayer? *Strong's Concordance* says it is "to entreat or go to." Prayer, then, is the way we get to God, the way we communicate with Him, the way we hear from Him and He hears from us. It also includes our praise and worship directed to Him.

Because of this, prayer is to the spirit what breath is to the body. If you stop breathing, you can't live long—probably only a matter of seconds. And it's the same way with prayer. Stop praying long enough, and you'll die spiritually. That's all there is to it.

If we are cut off from the very source of life, what can we expect? This is the reason that prayerlessness is such a grievous sin, one that God hates. It deeply saddens Him to see that His children no longer love Him as they once did and no longer delight to be with Him.

PRAYERLESSNESS IS A SIN IN EVERY RESPECT

Usually, when we think of sin, we think of overt acts of disobedience to God. Surely prayer could not be placed in that same category. Or could it?

First, prayerlessness is what we call a sin of omission. We can sin by doing something wrong, but we can also sin by not doing something we should be doing. The Bible makes this very clear when it says:

To him that knoweth to do good, and doeth it not, to him it is sin.

James 4:17

Sins of omission don't seem very serious to us, but because this particular sin of omission weakens your spiritual life, making you less useful to God and more vulnerable to spiritual loss, nothing could be more serious.

If nothing else moves you in this regard, consider the personal loss that can come to you through prayerlessness. Look at it from a selfish viewpoint, if you will. Prayerlessness will clearly rob you of many of the good things God has in store for you. Is that serious enough for you? May the Lord bring each of us to repentance and renewal in this matter so that we can not only live the abundant life He has ordained for us here, but also further His kingdom on the earth.

Prayerlessness, however, is not just a sin of omission. God has called us to pray for many things specifically, and when we fail to do that, we're neglecting our responsibility and directly disobeying our heavenly Father. This grieves His heart and puts at risk our future relationship with Him.

Webster's Dictionary defines *neglect* as "to omit by carelessness or by design; to ignore or disregard; to fail to care for or attend to." When you fail to obey God in His commands concerning your prayer life, you signal to Him not only that you are careless about the matters of your soul, but also that you have decided to ignore and disregard His commands. You're not willing to attend to His business in your life.

No wonder God takes this sin so seriously! You should too, for it can lead to your spiritual death.

Prayerlessness also makes you unavailable to God. He can't use people who fail to communicate with Him on a regular basis. How can you know the will of God for your life today if you haven't asked Him? How can you even know Him without the benefit of regular intimate communication with Him?

It's one thing to know someone from a distance, but it's quite another thing to know them intimately. I may feel that I know a certain popular preacher because I've seen them on television or been in one of their meetings, but do they know who I am or have we carried on a personal conversation? That's a different question entirely.

God knows those who know Him. This is the reason He declares to some, *"I never knew you"*:

And then will I profess unto them, I never knew you: depart from me, ye that work iniquity.

Matthew 7:23

Prayerlessness is a serious sin because it says to God that you now have very little love left for Him. You may well protest that point, but the truth is that if you loved Him more, you would also love to talk to Him. When you love someone, you enjoy communicating with them, and you take whatever time is necessary for it.

It's communication on every level that brings people together. If you and I were friends, and I hadn't seen you for a long time, I might have to say, "We used to be good friends. In fact, there was a time that we talked every day. But we're not very close anymore." The difference would be obvious.

Are there "good friends" who don't speak to each other for years at a time? I don't think so. In the same way, maybe you *used* to know God. But if you're not communicating with Him on a regular basis now, can you still say that you know Him?

Maybe you knew God's heart at one time, but is that still true? If you just show up once a week at His house and wave at Him from afar, that doesn't sound like love to me. It's never difficult or cumbersome to talk with someone you love.

PRAYERLESSNESS GRIEVES THE HEART OF GOD

Samuel Chadwick once said: "The crying need of the church is her laziness after God. The church needs nothing other than prayer because everything else follows prayer."[1]

Andrew Murray, the great man of prayer himself, said, "The sin of prayerlessness is proof that the life of God and the soul is in deadly sickness and weakness."[2]

E. M. Bounds, a man of prayer and a teacher on prayer, has said, "Prayer, much prayer, is the price of the anointing. Prayer, much prayer, is the sole condition of keeping it. Without this unceasing prayer, the anointing never comes. Without perseverance in prayer, the anointing, like manna overkept, breeds worms."[3]

It isn't how much I prayed last night. It's how much I've prayed since I got up this morning. God has said that His mercies are *"new [fresh] every morning"*:

It is of the Lord's mercies that we are not consumed, because his compassions fail not. They are new every morning.

Lamentations 3:22-23

We need to wake up thanking God for His mercies, thanking Him that we were able to sleep, that we had no pain in our bodies, and that we still have a sound mind. He kept us all night when hell could have destroyed us.

Praying people always have exciting things to talk about.

⚜

We need to wake up thanking God for being our Guide for the day, for walking with us and protecting us. We should thank Him all day long. Only praying lips are anointed lips.

Prayerlessness grieves the heart of God because a prayerless person is a carnal person. You can talk to some people for a few minutes and sense whether or not they've been in recent contact with God. If what comes out of their mouth is only foolishness, that's a good indication of prayerlessness.

Praying people always have exciting things to talk about. They can't wait to tell you what their prayers have wrought. They're expectant people because they have many petitions outstanding, and they can hardly wait to see what God will do next.

The Holy Spirit is the spirit of prayer, and one of His functions is to pray for us and with us. But when we become prayerless, He is grieved and often retreats. Some Christians suddenly wake up one day to find that the Holy Spirit is no longer with them. They used to speak in tongues now and again, but they haven't used this gift in a while now. Should the Spirit stay around if you display no need of Him in your daily life?

PRAYERLESSNESS IS A BLATANT DISREGARD OF THE WILL OF GOD

Prayerlessness is a blatant disregard of the will of God. It is rebelliousness against Him and against His will for your life. Paul wrote to his spiritual son Timothy:

68

I exhort therefore, that, first of all, supplications, prayers, intercessions, and giving of thanks, be made for all men; for kings, and for all that are in authority; that we may lead a quiet and peaceable life in all godliness and honesty. For this is good and acceptable in the sight of God our Saviour; who will have all men to be saved, and to come unto the knowledge of the truth.

1 Timothy 2:1-4

Jesus himself instructed those who would follow Him to pray for souls (for evangelism, for missions). He said:

The harvest truly is great, but the labourers are few: pray ye therefore the Lord of the harvest, that he would send forth labourers into his harvest.

Luke 10:2

We even have a model prayer recorded in Scripture, and Jesus used it to teach us the proper approaches to talking with God. We call it The Lord's Prayer, but it might better be called The Disciples' Prayer.

In this prayer, Jesus even told us how to approach God:

Our Father, which art in heaven.

Matthew 6:9

He is our Father, and we come to Him based on the Father/child relationship.

Jesus taught us that we should approach God with praise:

Hallowed by thy name.

Matthew 6:9

When it comes to making specific petitions, a major part of our prayer should be that His kingdom come and His will be done:

Thy kingdom come. Thy will be done in earth, as it is in heaven.

Matthew 6:10

It is much later in this model prayer that Jesus shows us how to approach God with our specific personal needs. But when we pray at all, these days, it's usually with just the opposite approach. We only pray for our own circle of friends and family and our own immediate needs, and we often do that without much preliminary praise. This is clearly selfish praying.

The kingdom of God goes much deeper than our little circle of friends and family members. We're part of the greatest family on earth, and the members of our family extend around the world. We may never see many of our brothers and sisters, but they're part of us nevertheless, and they need and deserve our prayers.

Somewhere, far across vast oceans, someone has been imprisoned for preaching the truth. They might never get out of that place alive if you fail to intercede for them. And yet, when we pray at all, we're still praying for mundane things.

Evangelists and missionaries in many places are toiling with very little thanks or help, somewhere people are dying of starvation, and some are being violated, and yet we go on with our pitiful selfish prayers—or none at all. May God help us.

The Scriptures teach us to pray for *"all that are in authority"* (1 Timothy 2:2). This includes both secular authority and spiritual authority. We should all pray for the public officials who are making decisions for our community, state and nation, and we should all pray for our pastors and other ministry officials. This is known as the ministry of intercession. Sadly, ours is usually the ministry of personal petition, when we even bother to pray at all.

Most modern American Christians know nothing of "praying through." We get up in the morning, quickly ask the Lord to bless us and ours, and then we're off to our activities of the day. "Praying through" means that you get God's heart, and then you stay in His presence, travailing in prayer, until the answer comes.

In previous generations, it was not uncommon at all for children to overhear their parents crying out to God. When Lawrence and I first got married, we had a neighbor who lived across the street from us, and we heard her praying every single night. My own mother-in-law was a person who cried out to God aloud, and we often overheard her praying for hours at a time, and my mother was always a strong woman of prayer as well.

> *When we're determined to "pray through," we're never rushed to "get through" with our prayers.*

When we're determined to "pray through," we're never rushed to "get through" with our prayers. We're willing to stay right there, and we want to stay right there, until the victory comes. Today, when people pray at all, they keep looking at their watch. "Is my fifteen minutes up yet?" they want to know. "Oh, no. I've only prayed for thirteen minutes. I still have two more minutes to go." But that's not "praying through."

When you "pray through," you won't want to stop praying. You'll begin to see things as God sees them. You may even cry out like Isaiah, and say, "Lord, if You need someone to send, send me. I know that I'm not worthy, but I'm willing." Prayerlessness does just the opposite.

71

JESUS CLEARLY EXPECTED HIS DISCIPLES TO PRAY

Jesus clearly expected that those who loved Him and chose to follow Him, thus becoming His disciples, would want to pray. He said, *"when you pray"* (Matthew 6:5), never *if you pray*. By our prayers, we show that we really love Him, and we show that we really love others. And what do we show by our lack of prayer?

The early disciples had the benefit of walking and talking physically with our Lord, and He even taught them the need to commune with the Father. How much more we need to pray today!

If we fail to pray, how can we discover the heartbeat of Jesus? It's worth discovering. When you've discovered it, you'll find that it's much bigger than your own. Prayerfulness makes you a bigger person, but prayerlessness makes you selfish.

When my daughter Julie left the church at the age of eighteen, I did a foolish thing. I said to God, "I'll never preach again. If I can't even convince my own children to live for You, how could I ever convince others? I quit!"

That was a very selfish prayer. I was hurting so much that all I could see was my own little world. But God was very gracious to me that day, and He spoke something that left me staggering: "If you're more interested in her soul than you are in anybody else's, I can't use you anyway." If I couldn't rejoice over someone else's child being saved, just as I would over my own, then I didn't have God's heart.

When we have God's heart, we rejoice when others are healed, just as if we had been healed ourselves. We have just begun to know God's heart, and we all have a lot to learn in this regard. What are we waiting for? Cast off prayerlessness, and get your soul on fire for God once again.

PRAYERLESSNESS SMOTHERS THE LIFE OUT OF US

It's a scary thing when a person experiences a shortness of breath. They feel like they're dying—even if they're not. And all too often, they actually are dying.

For instance, those who experience a blockage of the arteries and require bypass surgery (or, better yet, healing from God), first experience shortness of breath. Before long, it's a struggle for them just to walk up a few steps. This is a very serious condition, and if they don't get help, they may die.

That's how serious this condition of prayerlessness is for any individual and for the church as a whole. As we have seen, when prayerlessness invades our world, we're being cut off from the source of all life. So it's no wonder that prayerless people often stop going to church. It's a struggle for them just to stay alive. No wonder they stop going to prayer meetings! They're struggling for life itself.

...when prayerlessness invades our world, we're being cut off from the Source of all life.

Those who have life are eager for the church doors to open. They love to attend special conferences and retreats. They love to travel to other cities and other states to hear good preaching. They make great sacrifices and extend themselves to do it, and they love every minute of it. It's never too much of a burden for them.

But when you can't breathe, everything becomes more difficult. Not only can't you run; you can hardly walk. Some can't even crawl. And the saddest thing of all is that they sit idly by as what little life they still have ebbs out of them. It's time to cry out to God before it's too late.

PRAYERLESSNESS ROBS US OF MANY BENEFITS

One of the most serious ways in which prayerlessness robs us is in the area of God's guidance for our lives. If we no longer have His guidance, we may be stumbling around in the dark, going nowhere fast and not even know it.

Prayerlessness also robs us of God's power in our lives. We need His hand reaching out to meet our every need, and when that hand is absent, we're in serious trouble.

To me, one of the worst things about prayerless Christians is that they are so selfish. And that's understandable. When we don't feel God's heart, we cannot help but become selfish in our prayers.

The Christian life is to be lived for others, and Christ set the example for us. The Word of God teaches us:

Pray one for another ... .

James 5:16

Life is about more than you. But if you fail in this regard, you're not alone. The life of many Christians has become something of a swamp. The river of God's life is coming into it, but nothing goes out. Learning to pray unselfishly will release fresh water into your life and bring you many other benefits.

Prayerlessness underlies many evils in the church and robs us of many of the blessings God intended for our lives. It is time to put an end to it.

WE EASILY FORGET

We all start out well in prayer, but somewhere along the line we forget how important it is to us, and we begin to neglect it. Some years ago, when our children were still living at home, the Lord impressed on me that, as a family, we needed to meet downstairs every night at eleven o'clock and pray. We did that for many years. Then, when the children were gone from our home, and it was usually only Lawrence and myself or perhaps one other person, I decided that I would just do my praying in my room. The Lord quickly convicted me. "I told you to do that," He said. "Did I tell you to stop it?"

He hadn't. I had taken it upon myself to stop, and it hadn't been His will. We resumed the prayers, and great blessings came as a result.

Why is it that some people can watch television for hours, and yet they don't have time to pray? Why is it that they can talk on the telephone for hours to a friend, and yet they don't have time to pray? Something's not right when this is the case.

There are people we don't like to talk to on the telephone, and when they call, we want to get them off the line as quickly as possible. I sometimes have that experience, just like everyone else does. But when my children call or Lawrence calls from out of town, I'm never in a hurry to get the conversation over with and get them off of the line. I want to know everything they have to say because I love them. Why, then, can't we give God more time in prayer? Prayerlessness, I'm afraid, says, "My love for God has diminished or died altogether."

"How can you pray a whole hour?" some people ask. Well, how do they talk on the telephone for a whole hour? How do they watch television for a whole hour? Or two? Or three? As people who depend upon God for everything, we simply cannot afford to forget Him—even for a moment.

IS PRAYERLESSNESS JUST A WEAKNESS?

Some find it too strong a word to call prayerlessness a sin. They would rather label it a weakness, an oversight, or a result of busyness. But when we, for any reason, neglect to do what we know we should be doing, it's a sin.

I know that people get busy, often too busy. Even ministers get so busy working for God that they don't have time to pray, but that doesn't make it right. A classic Bible example should speak to us all in this regard.

Mary and Martha were sisters who both loved Jesus. He was close to their whole family and often stopped to see them when He was anywhere near Jerusalem, for they lived just outside the city in the little town of Bethany. Later, Jesus would weep over their departed brother Lazarus and then raise him from the dead.

One day, when Jesus was visiting their home, Martha was busy fixing His dinner and otherwise preparing for Him to have an enjoyable stay with them. Mary would normally have been helping her sister, but she was so intrigued by what Jesus had to say that she delayed and sat at His feet longer than she had intended.

This bothered Martha so much that she approached Jesus about it. Did He not care that Mary was neglecting her household duties? Shouldn't He admonish her to do what was right and proper?

Jesus' answer to Martha that day is enlightening:

And Jesus answered and said unto her, Martha, Martha, thou art careful and troubled about many things: but one thing is needful: and Mary hath chosen that good part, which shall not be taken away from her.

Luke 10:41-42

Martha was not wrong to be concerned about the earthly comfort of Jesus. But Mary had chosen to focus on the eternal, and Jesus praised her for that.

This matter of having enough time to pray is not a question of clergy versus laity. All of us need to pray. Each of us, whatever our place in the church, depends on the Lord for life, and we cannot afford to be separated from Him at any moment or for any reason.

PRAYER MAKES ALL THE DIFFERENCE

An interesting Bible story shows us what a difference it makes when we've spent time with God. Some Jewish exorcists saw Paul using the name of Jesus effectively and decided that they would try it themselves. The results were very different than they had imagined. The Scriptures declare:

Then certain of the vagabond Jews, exorcists, took upon them to call over them which had evil spirits the name of the Lord Jesus, saying, We adjure you by Jesus whom Paul preacheth. And there were seven sons of one Sceva, a Jew, and chief of the priests, which did so. And the evil spirit answered and said, Jesus I know, and Paul I know; but who are ye? And the man in whom the evil spirit was leaped on them, and overcame them, and prevailed against them, so that they fled out of that house naked and wounded. And this was known to all the Jews and Greeks also dwelling at Ephesus; and fear fell on them all, and the name of the Lord Jesus was magnified.

Acts 19:13-17

Devils know when you've been with Jesus, and they fear only those who pray. That means that only people who pray have power with God. This is why God's Word exhorts us:

Men ought always to pray, and not to faint.

Luke 18:1

This phrase *"not to faint"* means not to quit, not to give up. Keep on praying until the answer comes. And if *"men ought always to pray,"* then prayerlessness is a serious sin that we need to deal with and overcome.

PRAYERLESSNESS REVEALS A LACK OF SPIRITUAL DESIRE

These are all valid enough reasons for us to recognize the problem of prayerlessness and work on it. But, to me, the most dreadful thing about prayerlessness is that it reveals a lack of spiritual desire on our part.

It's not enough just to talk to God in your car on the way to work. That's well and good, and I do it every time I get in my car. People must think I'm crazy as they pass me by and notice that I seem to be talking to myself.

Recently, this has improved somewhat. So many people now have cell phones that people probably think that I'm talking into one. That may make me look less strange to those passing by.

I love to pray in my car as I drive, but just praying as you drive along, as good as that is, is not enough. You need to get alone with Him and have more extended times of intimacy with Him—just the two of you with no distractions. God will never speak to us during halftime of a game or during a commercial break in some television program.

During your intimate times with God, you can't be worried about the telephone ringing, and you have to ignore the doorbell. He's more important than anyone who might call you on the telephone or ring your doorbell. Listen to Him, and let Him listen to you, and you'll get to know each other better.

One of the major causes of the breakup of marriages these days is a lack of communication. The wife complains, "He works all the time, so we never have any time together."

His answer usually is, "Well, I'm working for you, trying to pay for the house you live in and the car you drive." But that's not a legitimate excuse. She didn't marry a house or a car. She married a man, so she needs time alone with him. If they have no intimate time together, what kind of marriage is it? And if most of us spent as little intimate time with our marriage partner as we do with God, our marriage wouldn't last very long. If intimacy with our bride or groom is important to us, how much more important is intimacy with our heavenly Bridegroom?

A more apt comparison might be that of those who are engaged to be married. How often do engaged couples speak to each other? Would it be enough to meet a few minutes now and then or to catch a few minutes of phone conversation a day? And yet that's the way we treat God.

Sometimes I weep for Him. My heart is broken as I feel what He must feel. He does so much for us, and yet we go about our day as if He didn't even exist. Did all of those wonderful things just happen on their own? Did they happen just because we're so intelligent and wonderful? I don't think so.

Too many times, we don't even stop to think where all of our blessings have come from. They're tokens of God's love for us, signs of His intense caring. And He wants to do much more for us. Jesus said:

Fear not, little flock; for it is your Father's good pleasure to give you the kingdom.

Luke 12:32

We need to repent for our coldness and ingratitude to God and ask Him to forgive us. Then we need to do better in the future. Prayerlessness simply has to go.

START DEVELOPING YOUR PRAYER LIFE NOW

Real prayer cannot begin the day you're told that you have cancer or you have to undergo open-heart surgery, and it can't begin the day you're served with divorce papers. It takes time to develop a relationship with God, just as it does with any other person. And you can't just use Him like you do a spare tire.

Spare tires are important, and we all want to know that we have one. Any time we experience a flat with one of our four main tires, we get out the spare and put it on, and it serves us well until the other tire is repaired. When we have a flat tire, we're awfully glad to find that we have a viable spare. But soon enough, we put the spare tire back in the trunk and forget about it until the next crisis comes along. When things are going well, we don't need it.

Is God just a spare tire to you? Do you use Him only when you have an emergency? Speaking for myself, God has done so much for me already that if He never did another thing for me, still my lips would have to continually praise Him. I can't wait for some emergency to come along to begin building my prayer life. I have to do it now.

God fully intended for prayer to be the great power by which His church operates.

Building up your prayer life is a lot like doing weight training. You may not see the results immediately. Doing one session of weight training and then staring into the mirror to see the benefit would be foolish. It takes a while. Within six weeks, the change can be obvious and dramatic.

And the longer you do weight training the easier it becomes. Something that seems heavy for you at the beginning will eventually feel very light, and you'll be able to lift more and more. When we first begin to pray, we may receive only power to heal headaches, but when we persevere in prayer, the power to heal cancer will come. Once you've developed a life of prayer, demons will have to obey you. Your very presence will send them scurrying.

God fully intended for prayer to be the great power by which His church operates. We can organize and reorganize, but nothing much will happen. We can do things that bring in big crowds, but nothing much will happen. It takes intense prayer to bring revival.

Many churches have suspended their prayer meetings simply because no one comes, or a very few come. I've seen it happen time after time. When we first begin a prayer meeting, many people get excited and attend the early sessions, but as time goes on, fewer and fewer come. There are other demands on their time. There are other things that are "more fun" than prayer. Or they decide to do their praying at home and avoid the trip to church. Whatever the reason, one after another, they drop out, until we're left with a faithful few.

I know that many people commute to church these days, some from thirty minutes away, some from an hour away, and some from even farther. When they say they can't attend prayer meetings, it seems to make sense, and sometimes it does. But what about all of those who live much closer to the church? Even they can't attend a prayer meeting? This just shows us how unimportant prayer has become to many of us. To most, prayer is not worth any great sacrifice at all.

If would be different if the people not attending prayer meetings were praying at home, but they're not. They're watching television, or they're out shopping or doing other things they enjoy more. All of us do what's important to us. Do you enjoy spending time with God?

I know what it is to be busy. In fact, I can't imagine that any-one could be busier than I am. Still, I refuse to neglect my prayer life because I know how very important it is to me personally and also to my ministry. I never miss a prayer meeting at our church if I'm in town. Everything about my life hinges on prayer, so nothing can be allowed to displace it in importance.

John Wesley once said, "I pray two hours every morning. That is if I don't have a lot to do. If I have a lot to do for that day, then I pray three hours."

Abraham Lincoln said, "If I had eight hours to chop down a tree, I'd spend six of those hours sharpening my axe."[4] That's what we all need to do, spend some time sharpening our blade. Then it will be much easier to get things accomplished in life.

Determine today that you will avoid the deadly sin of prayerlessness. It represents a dying desire, and there is an inseparable link between your desire and your destiny.

ENDNOTES

1. Bounds, E. M. *The Possibilities of Prayer*. Grand Rapids, MI: Baker Publishing Group, 1992

2. Murray, Andrew, *Prayer Life*. Grand Rapids, MI: Zondervan, 1999

3. Bounds, E. M., *Power through Prayer*. Grand Rapids, MI: Baker Publishing Group, 1991

4. http://en.thinkexist.com/quotes/abraham_lincoln/

Chapter 5

KILL THE KING: SATAN'S PLAN OF ATTACK AGAINST YOUR DESIRE

So the king of Israel [Ahab] and Jehoshaphat the king of Judah went up to Ramoth-gilead.

But the king of Syria commanded his thirty and two captains that had rule over his chariots, saying, Fight neither with small nor great, save only with the king of Israel.

And a certain man drew a bow at a venture, and smote the king of Israel between the joints of the harness: wherefore he said unto the driver of his chariot, Turn thine hand, and carry me out of the host; for I am wounded.

And the battle increased that day: and the king was stayed up in his chariot against the Syrians, and died at even: and the blood ran out of the wound into the midst of the chariot.

1 Kings 22:29, 31, 34-35

You have to give the king of Syria credit. He had a great battle plan when he went out to war against the kings of Israel and Judah. He instructed his men to ignore, for the most part, the opposing generals, lieutenants, and captains and go after King Ahab himself. They should attempt to kill him early in the battle. This would quickly demoralize the enemy and insure victory over them. What a smart king!

Ahab also recognized what a great strategy this was, and when he was wounded early in the battle by a well-placed arrow, he asked not to be taken away from the scene of the battle. Instead, his driver pulled to the side and propped the king up in his chariot. All day long, as the battle raged, the king's lifeblood drained out of him onto the floor of his chariot, but he stubbornly refused to retreat from the scene. If the enemy (or even his own men) knew that he was dying, the battle would be over.

That evening, the king died anyway, and the battle was over.

SATAN HAS A GREAT BATTLE PLAN

What a great strategy: kill the king, and the armies will be demoralized and scatter in confusion! When I read this passage again a few years ago, it suddenly dawned on me that this is Satan's strategy against the church today. If he can rob us of our Source of life, he can gradually weaken us until we no longer pose any threat to him or his kingdom.

What is that one thing upon which our victory depends? It can only be our prayer life, our connection to the Source of everything we need. And if Satan can cut that connection, he can easily defeat us.

Prayer is our umbilical cord, attaching us to the life of God. Prayer is our life-support system, pumping His life into us when we have none of our own. If we can stay hooked up to the system, we can live. But if that connection is disturbed for any length of time, that will soon be the end of us.

USING AHAB'S DELAYING TACTICS

What King Ahab did when he was wounded was not a wise thing. In fact, it was just a delaying tactic, and it worked only for a few hours. Because he had himself propped up, he looked to most people as if he was still alert and ready to aid in the battle. But the truth was that his life force was slowly being drained from him, and he wouldn't last long.

In the same way, it may seem wise to some in the church today to pretend that everything is all right when it's not, but the pretense can't last long. Soon enough, the truth will be known. If your life has become prayerless, you may successfully hide that fact for a while. But eventually the truth will come out.

Some people have propped themselves up, and they're still singing in the choir. Some are propped up at the pulpit. Some are propped up as teachers in our Sunday school classes. But the life is draining from them, and they will soon be dead. Then everyone will know the truth.

"I wanted to be there in church last Sunday night," some say, "but I just couldn't seem to make it." When I hear people say that, I pray for them. They're dying and may not even realize what's happening.

You see some people coming in the door, and you can tell that attending services has become a drudgery for them. When I see that, I pray for them. They're in imminent danger of death.

STRUGGLING TO REMAIN UPRIGHT

As his strength ebbed away, remaining upright in his chariot must have become more and more of a strain for King Ahab. The amazing thing is that he was able to carry out the sham for an entire day. By evening, he could hold out no longer. His strength was gone. He died, and everyone soon knew the truth about him.

When prayer has become nothing more than a habit, we're in trouble.

When prayer has become nothing more than a habit, we're in trouble. When prayer has been boiled down to a three-minute recitation to God before we go to sleep each night, we're in trouble. When prayer becomes simply a means of salving our conscience, we're in trouble.

Prayerlessness affects the individual, and then it begins to affect the whole church. Programs without prayer are just programs. There's no power in them. But even though we feel that something has become simply a habit, what can we do? We have to "have church," so we sing the songs and pray the prayers, and because our faith can no longer produce anything of consequence, we resort to imitating what we did in the past. The Scriptures call this *"a form of godliness"* (2 Timothy 3:5) and shows us that God rejects it.

Just going through the motions is never acceptable to God. His church is not an organization; it's a living, growing, breathing organism. And it depends on Him for its life. Pretending just won't do.

When prayer dies, it's not long before the gifts of the Spirit stop manifesting in our midst, the supernatural disappears, and there's no more prophecy and discernment. When prayer dies, preaching suffers. The truth is suddenly replaced with comforting platitudes. No wonder many no longer preach about miracles! They never see them these days, so how could they preach about them?

Just as happened with King Ahab, Satan struck a master blow to America when, through the court system, he successfully barred prayer from our classrooms. Today, those same classrooms are full of hell and not nearly enough education. Our children are now involved in drugs, alcohol, sex, and even murder. School used to be a place of education, but now it may be a place of execution. What can we expect? The end of those who forget God will never be a pretty one:

> *The wicked shall be turned into hell, and all the nations that forget God.*
>
> Psalm 9:17

Cry out to God today to deliver America from prayerlessness.

WITHDRAW IMMEDIATELY AND SEEK HELP

When Ahab realized that he was wounded, he should have withdrawn himself and/or his army immediately and sought help. It was only because he was a stubborn and arrogant man that he could not bring himself to do it. He simply had to act like everything was all right and go on with the planned battle.

That was a very foolish thing to do. When you're wounded, that's not the time to act like nothing has happened. Get help right away. This is a matter of life and death. Draw aside and get the assistance you need before it's too late.

This is not the time to be going to a movie with a friend. You flip through a hundred and eighty channels on your television, but nothing seems to satisfy. You go the refrigerator, but can't find anything you want to eat. All the while your spirit is crying out for help, saying, "Take me to my God! I'm hungry. I'm thirsty. I need a fresh touch from heaven. Take me to my God." Hurry to God before your life drains out of you, and it's too late.

OUR BUSYNESS PLAYS INTO SATAN'S HANDS

The busyness of our modern lifestyle plays into Satan's hands because it's not conducive to prayer. We live in a shake-and-bake, heat-and-eat, brown-and-serve, hurry-up-and-wait society, and we rush about all day from one activity to another. Then we get up the next day and start the same race all over again. In this context, even a three-minute prayer seems to be a sacrifice, but it's not enough.

Sometimes I preach several times or even many times a week, and it would be very easy to think that because I'm working for God I have no time for prayer. But I could never afford to do that. I can't take the chance that my lifeblood will be drained from me, and I might lose the battle. I must insist on having precious time alone with God.

As I noted before, some people actually get so busy working for Him that they have no time to spend with Him. Does that make any sense?

Whenever this happens in our lives, sometimes the Lord has to allow trouble to come to us so that we'll seek Him. What a way to get a person's attention! And yet the only time some people talk to God is when they're in trouble. So He has to do it that way—for the good of their soul.

A few years ago, I became familiar with the case of a prominent pastor who became involved in prescription drug abuse and illicit sex and eventually took his own life. Amazingly, his widow told me that he had spent eight to ten hours every day studying for his sermons. She came to the conclusion that, although he had spent that much time preparing to speak, he had actually spent very little personal time with God. She likened it to a politician preparing for an important stump speech.

Think about that. Her husband was preparing to feed others, but he was not being fed himself. Nothing can ever replace prayer. Nothing!

Going to church is not enough. Paying your tithes is not enough. Satan doesn't care if you do those things. He just doesn't want you to have intimate contact with the God of the universe. He knows that prayerlessness on your part can give him the victory quicker than anything else, and he loves to sit back and watch you bleed. He loves it when the king is dying. Then he can have his way. Run to God and put prayer back in its rightful place in your life, as king.

THE VALUE OF SPENDING TIME IN GOD'S PRESENCE

All of us, ministers and lay people alike, need time in God's presence. In His presence, there is *"fullness of joy"*:

91

Thou wilt show me the path of life: in thy presence is fulness of joy; at thy right hand there are pleasures for evermore.

Psalm 16:11

Joy is equal to *"strength"*:

The joy of the Lord is your strength.

Nehemiah 8:10

When you linger in God's presence, wounds are healed, and all that you need for life is poured into you. Your flabby muscles are strengthened, and suddenly you become a threat to Satan and his kingdom. He will do absolutely anything to prevent that from happening. He doesn't want you hooked up to that lifeline. He wants to see you drained of life so that you're no longer a threat to him.

If you take prayer out of the preacher, all you have left is a person who knows how to make a good speech. If you take prayer out of the Sunday school teacher, all you have left is someone who can present a good lesson. It takes an altar of prayer to make an anointed man or woman of God. God is calling us to cast off this deadly sin of prayerlessness.

WE WERE CREATED FOR CONSTANT COMMUNICATION

God created us for constant communication with Him. After He had created Adam and Eve, He came down in the cool of the day and walked and talked with them. Can you imagine God coming to your house one morning, knocking on your door, and saying, "Come on, let's have a walk so that we can talk some things over"? Wouldn't that be wonderful?

Would you ever dare to say to Him, "I'm too busy. Let me get the kids off to school first. Then, as soon as I finish the dishes and my conference call to the office, we can talk"?

God created us for fellowship, and yet modern man has become too busy to have the kind of fellowship with God that He envisioned when He created us. In this way, the very reason for our creation has been thwarted by our own willfulness and coldness of spirit.

"I'm too busy," may sound legitimate, but we're all creatures of habit, and we can develop good habits and bad habits. "I don't have time," is just an excuse. We have time for what we want to have time for. Admit it and ask God to help you reserve more time for Him.

SO WHERE DOES THE PROBLEM LIE?

I wasted many years of my life trying to blame my failures on someone else or something else. "If only I hadn't married a man who was so dedicated to business," I thought many times. "If only I had gone on to get more education, perhaps then I could have done something more for God." What a waste of time this kind of thinking proved to be! When I got serious with God in prayer, He showed me where my problem was. It was in me.

I had two neighbors whose husbands sometimes traveled with Lawrence, and I would spend a lot of time with them. Although they were morally upright, they were not churchgoing people, and we had little in common.

I went to church on Sundays and Wednesdays and took my children with me, but otherwise my spiritual life seemed to be going nowhere. "Why aren't You using me more, Lord," I would ask Him almost every morning. I knew that I was called, but my calling seemed to be stalled.

When I finally saw what the problem was, I was shocked. I was like King Ahab, dying, and just propped up for the sake of appearance. I needed to make some major changes in my life.

I was like King Ahab, dying, and just propped up for the sake of appearance.

One of the first things I had to do was to be more careful about the company I kept. Too much time with my friends and not enough time with God was holding me back. I had to make a hard decision about my friends.

When the space shuttle launches from Cape Canaveral, it's sent off toward its destination by booster rockets. At a certain altitude, those booster rockets and the fuel tanks that supply them must be jettisoned, and then the space shuttle can attain earth orbit.

If, for some reason, the shuttle would be unable to loose itself from those large fuel tanks and the booster rockets, it would crash. It's only by the act of freeing itself from that extra burden that the shuttle can attain the weightlessness of outer space.

There are some people in our lives whom we can hold on to for just so long. Then we have to let them go. They were there for a reason. The Bible says:

Iron sharpeneth iron; so a man sharpeneth the countenance of his friend.

Proverbs 27:17

If we are willing to break some unhealthy relationships, God will give us better ones. Thinking back to those former times, and considering the kind of people I now call my friends—the Juanita Bynams, the Paula Whites, the Rod Parsleys, the T. D. Jakes of this world—look where God has brought me from.

If I had insisted on holding on to my old friends, I would still be doing the same old things today. There are some people and some things that we have to let go of if we are to make any progress in life. And our choices in this regard reflect the depth of our spiritual desire (or lack of it).

It's nice to spend time with a friend every Friday night, but it's much more wonderful to spend time with God. When people come to me and tell me they want to do something for Him, I ask them what they're doing differently these days to make that happen. Usually, the answer is, "I don't know. Nothing, I guess." And that explains why they're still going nowhere.

God wants to be pursued, and halfhearted efforts will not do. You can't expect to give God your leftovers, and then ask Him to bless you as you desire. Some people stay out with their friends until all hours of the night, then they come home, read a few verses from the Bible and say a few lines of a dry prayer, and expect God to bless everything they do. It doesn't work that way. You must develop a prayer life. That's not just a few lines of a prayer or a prayer meeting. A prayer life is a life rooted in prayer.

WHAT A DAILY LIFELINE TO GOD WILL DO FOR YOU

When we have developed a prayer life, we don't have to call a dozen people about every problem we encounter in life.

We're hooked up to the heavenly lifeline, and nothing is hindering the flow of blessing between us and God.

This is the reason it's so important to repent quickly when we know that we have displeased God in any way. This keeps the window of blessing always open. Sin can too easily separate us from God.

Don't let anything keep you from prayer. We may go for a day or two without prayer, and no one will know, but when we go four or five days without it, our spouse and children will know. And when we've gone a week or two without it, everyone will know. You may sit propped up for a while, but as the life drains from you, eventually you will collapse, and everyone will become painfully aware of your failure.

There is a thrill to be experienced in the presence of God. Don't miss it. One night Lawrence and I were out visiting some friends, and it began to get late. By the time we got home, it was already eleven thirty. I told Lawrence, "You've made me miss my appointment with the Lord." But I was just kidding. I knew that we would pray anyway, even though we were late getting started.

When we arrived at the house, my good friend Arlene, who lives with us, had the lights down low and the music playing. As I walked in, I felt a wonderful presence of the Lord that brought tears to my eyes. Nothing can compare to God's presence.

I look forward to my quiet times with the Lord. How wonderful, when it's just me and Him! When people tell me that they never hear from God, I know immediately that they have no proper prayer life. No Christian can afford to go any length of time without hearing His voice.

When we fall out of love with Jesus and prayer suddenly becomes a drudgery, a constant struggle, a dread rather than a delight, Satan is delighted. He's not so worried when we memorize the Bible. He knows it too ... a lot better than most of us do. His one goal is to cut us off from communication with the Author of the Word of Life. Don't let it happen.

PRAYERLESSNESS IS A CHOICE

Prayer is something no one can take from you unless you let them do it. It might be possible for someone to take your Bible away from you, but you could still pray. In the extreme, someone could even cut out your tongue, but that wouldn't stop you from communicating with God through your spirit. If you stop praying, it's because you wanted to stop praying.

As ministers, we are confronted every single day of our lives with people's needs. We need to be able to say to them, "Let me pray for you," and then we need to instantly touch heaven for them.

When this happens, any time of night or day, we should not have to call the Lord up or pull Him down. He must be right here with us at all times, and we must be in constant contact with Him. Prayer, therefore, should become, for each of us, as natural as breathing—and just as indispensable.

Some wait until they're too sick or in too much pain to start praying. But it's hard to pray under those conditions, and many never find help. If, on the other hand, you already know the Lord intimately, you can touch Him in a moment's time and be healed.

Why is it that the attendance at prayer meetings is the lowest of any service? I'm afraid it's because twenty-first century

Christians have made a conscious decision to give prayer a lower place of importance in their lives. And, of course, Satan is behind it all. He is determined to keep you from what he knows to be your lifeline. He wants to kill the king.

If he can keep you from praying, he has you like Ahab, wounded and powerless. The life is flowing out of you, and it's only a matter of time before you will be dead and gone. It's time for change. Stop chasing after things, and start pursuing God.

ISAIAH'S AWAKENING

As we saw, it didn't take long for King Ahab's dilemma to become apparent to all. You can only prop up a dead man for so long. After a while, he will begin to stink. A similar thing happened to Isaiah, and it brought a great awakening to his life.

When King Uzziah died, it brought about many changes. Isaiah went into the house of the Lord, and there he encountered the living God. The first thing he noticed was his own need:

Then said I, Woe is me! for I am undone; because I am a man of unclean lips, and I dwell in the midst of a people of unclean lips: for mine eyes have seen the King, the Lord of hosts.

Isaiah 6:5

Immediately, the Lord sent a seraphim to purge Isaiah. Then He demanded something of the man:

Also I heard the voice of the Lord, saying, Whom shall I send, and who will go for us? Then said I, Here am I; send me.

Isaiah 6:8

For those who experience God's presence, service is never a burden or a sacrifice. It's a privilege in which they take delight. People who have been in God's presence are eager to serve in the nursery, to usher, or to do anything else that's needed at the moment.

Isaiah was quick to respond to the Lord: *"Here am I; send me."* He wasn't worried about qualifications. The Lord's presence qualified him. This was his turnaround.

MY OWN AWAKENING

I remember every detail of the day things turned around in my own life. I had been shopping that day and I bought a new dress. When I got home, Jana saw the dress and said to me, "Mom, you already have a dress just like that." I couldn't imagine that she was right, but to prove her point, she went into my closet and came out holding the dress in question.

Sure enough, I had bought a dress exactly like one I already had in the closet. I was shocked. So this was what my life had become, an endless shopping spree? Without delay or pretense, I went into my bathroom, fell on my face before the Lord, and began to confess that I was the problem, not Lawrence, and not anyone else.

From that moment on, I determined, rather than trying to blame someone or something else for my failure, I would pursue the Lord as I knew I should have been pursuing Him all along. Whatever He wanted me to do, that's what I would do.

If it was teaching a Sunday-school class, I would become a Sunday-school teacher. If it was something else, I would do that. Most of all, I would spend time alone with God.

From that day on, whenever I had an urge to go shopping, I would pick up my Bible and begin to study it, and I would take the time to pray. With this, the Bible soon became my daily bread, and my time with God became my strength.

And many other things began to change. Within six months after I made that commitment and began that new kind of prayer life, Lawrence had a Damascus Road experience one day and was totally changed. I was, and still am, convinced that God would have dealt with him much sooner if I had gotten my own act together sooner. When I acted, God acted. That must mean that He's waiting for us, and the failure is ours, never His.

STOP BLAMING OTHERS

We use anything as an excuse: a divorce, an ex-spouse, a sibling, or something else, but in the end it all comes down to one thing. Do you love God and will you pursue Him above all else?

It's our nature to want to blame our lack on others. Adam blamed Eve, and she blamed the serpent. But if we lack, it's because we have not committed all to God. There can be no other reason. God will not judge you for the failure of others. He deals with you on the basis of your own relationship with Him.

Become obsessed with God, with His kingdom, with His will, and with His Word, and when you do, you'll find that *"all things work together for good"*:

And we know that all things work together for good to them that love God, to them who are the called according to his purpose.

Romans 8:28

If we expect to have this great promise fulfilled in our lives, then we also need to heed the biblical admonition:

Stand fast therefore in the liberty wherewith Christ hath made us free, and be not entangled again with the yoke of bondage.

Galatians 5:1

Be careful that your earthly relationships don't interfere with this most important relationship. Many are obsessed with the desire to get married to a wonderful person. They've been deceived by all the Hollywood hype into thinking that this will bring them fulfillment in life. It's time for us to stop living by Hollywood standards.

If you get married, it's not just to make you happy. A good marriage alone will not bring fulfillment to your soul. God has a higher purpose for your life, and you need to seek that higher purpose. Seek His kingdom first, and when you do that, the things you need will be added to you. God has promised to *"perfect that which concerneth [us]"*:

The Lord will perfect that which concerneth me.

Psalm 138:8

This being true, we don't have to worry about things. That's not our responsibility; God will do it. So relax. If you love Him, and you're called according to His purpose, you have nothing to worry about. As long as you're working for God's kingdom, how could He permit you to do without the things you need? His Word assures us that He knows what we need before we ask.

We're so worried about our earthly relationships that we often allow them to rob us of our spirituality. "He was my drinkin' buddy for as long as I can remember," some man might say. So he's reluctant to let his friend go. The result is that the life is sapped from him, and he dies. In the same way, old boyfriends and girlfriends often become snares for new believers.

Then we wonder why God isn't doing what He has promised to do. We received a prophecy, and it's not coming to pass (for some reason). It won't come to pass as long as we continue to put other people and other things before God. What you do in this regard will make it happen, or what you do in this regard will cause it not to happen.

WHAT HAPPENED TO US

The day Lawrence and I began pursuing God with all that was within us, our lives began to turn around dramatically. We went to church every time the doors were open. We arrived early and stayed late. We performed willingly and cheerfully anything that was asked of us. And God began to take care of us in ways we had not experienced before.

If you love God and are interested in His kingdom and His will, He'll do the same for you. But if you continue to live in the same old way day after day, week after week, and month after month, seeing the same old friends, entertaining the same old habits, seeing the same movies and reading the same books, playing the same games and living the same lifestyle, then don't expect God to do something different for you. You've made your choice.

Many Christians are sure that miracles ceased with the apostles, but the truth is that miracles cease when we stop praying. There's no substitute for prayer, and if Satan can succeed in killing your prayer life, then it's over.

This is even true for young people. A wise young person should insist on developing a prayer life. I sometimes think back and wonder what I might have done for the kingdom if I had given the Lord the fifteen years I wasted doing my own thing. If I had been in pursuit of God during those fifteen years like I have in the past twenty years, there's no telling what could have been accomplished.

Don't allow the things of life to crowd out your spirituality.

LIVES CLUTTERED WITH LEGITIMATE THINGS

Don't allow the things of life to crowd out your spirituality. Our modern lives are often cluttered with seemingly legitimate things. They may not be sins in themselves, but the sin is that they rob us of the time we need to spend with God.

When Joseph knocked on the door of the inn and asked for a room, he was given a very legitimate answer. There were no rooms available. He protested that his wife was about ready to give birth, but the answer was the same: "There is no room."

What could Joseph say? It was a legitimate answer. There was no room. In the very same way, our lives are often full of just such legitimacy. But can anything be legitimate when it takes God's place in our hearts and in our daily routine?

To say that you are prayerless might not be to say that there are other blatant sins in your life; it may be that there is simply no room for prayer. You work hard, and when you get home, you like to have time with your family. You have to eat, and you have to relax sometimes. Then it's time to go to bed, and the next day looks just like the last one.

You do go to church, but other than that limited time which you have successfully allotted for the Lord, He has been crowded out of your life. Then you wonder why sickness or financial trouble comes, and you're compelled to cry out to God. This may be the only way the Lord can get your attention.

He has already provided for your healing, and He has already provided for your financial rescue because He knows that there will be times when He will have to force you to need His intervention. Otherwise, His will is that you remain well and financially blessed.

DESIRING HIS PRESENCE

In recent years, I've traveled a lot in ministry, and Lawrence travels a lot with his business, and sometimes I get so hungry just to talk to him and hear him talk to me. He feels exactly the same way. Sometimes he says to me, "Can we just sit down for a few minutes. We haven't had time to talk in days. Can we just do nothing but talk for a while?"

We do it, and it's wonderful. How much more this should be true of us spending time with our Lord.

How long has it been since you talked to Him, really talked to Him, shared your heart with Him, and "loved on" Him? I'm not talking about asking God for things. In your most intimate times with Him, you won't be able to think of a single thing you need.

I used to sing an old song that said:

I've just come to talk to You, Lord.
I don't need anything.
I just want to thank You for all the other times
and all the things that You've done.

I want to know Your heart, Lord.
I want to know what You need.
What is Your need, God?

Did you know that God has needs? He has longings, just like we do. He seeks love, just like we do. He's waiting to meet with you today.

COME ASIDE

Come aside, saints of God, and put first things first. If you're guilty of neglecting prayer, Satan will drag you down very quickly. If you've been wounded, turn aside quickly and get help. Don't risk allowing your life to ebb out of you.

We're living in the midst of a pleasure-hungry society, and people all around us are rushing here and there to find satisfaction. Please don't be caught up in this trap and miss God. Listen to the cry of your heart and His.

We Christians sometimes get busy in religious activity— knocking on doors, handing out tracts, singing, and preaching. These are all good, but somehow prayer seems to get sacrificed. Many of those who attend our churches these days watch the clock, and if the preacher goes over thirty minutes, they get up and leave. They have somewhere to go, someone to meet, or something to eat. How sad! God is last on their list of important things to do, and they rarely seem to get to Him.

NOTHING COULD STOP JOHN FROM PRAYING

When the apostle John was exiled to the Isle of Patmos, they stripped him of everything he possessed. They were sure that he had been immobilized, but they forgot one thing. They couldn't stop him from praying. He was praying one Lord's Day when a wonderful revelation came to him:

I was in the Spirit on the Lord's day, and heard behind me a great voice, as of a trumpet, Saying... .

Revelation 1:10-11

Although they had stripped John of everything, even his physical sight, they were unable to cut off his direct link to heaven. Like John, I can say, "Take this whole world, but give me a life of prayer with the Lord. Let me ever cling to the horns of God's altar." How long has it been since you stayed on your knees until you knew that victory had come?

When the early disciples were imprisoned, they thanked God for the privilege to suffer for Him and then prayed that they would have boldness to continue. They had learned this life of prayer from Jesus himself. His custom was to rise early in the morning and go to a mountain where He could be alone with the Father. If the very Son of God had to pull himself aside to maintain life, how much more should we do the same?

Oh, it will be a struggle to fight your flesh day in and day out, because it doesn't want to pray. Satan is behind that fight. He knows that you can conquer him in every other area but this one. He knows that the man or woman who prays is a man or woman of God who will fulfill his or her purpose in God. Search your heart today to see how you can effectively spend more time with God in prayer.

One day I called a woman from our church on the telephone. Her daughter answered and said, "I'm sorry, Ms. Darlene, but my mother's in prayer, and I can't disturb her." I thought that was so wonderful that I fell down to give thanks to the Lord. Let that be you.

Someone interviewed our daughter Julie, and one of the questions they asked was, "Having been raised as a preacher's daughter, what's your fondest memory?" I imagine they were expecting her to say that she remembered meeting all the many famous preachers and singers who came to the church and our house, but I thought her answer was wonderful. "The thing I remember most," she said, "was going into Daddy's prayer closet while he was praying. I would climb up on his back and go to sleep there while he was seeking God." There could be no greater memory for any son or daughter.

Let me ask you today: If I came to your house and interviewed your children, would they be able to show me the place where you pray? Would they know what your regular prayer time was or even if you had one?

Church, let's get our list of important things in order. Let's make some necessary adjustments and find more time for God. Too many times, our heavenly Father calls, but no one answers. He speaks, but no one listens. His heart yearns, but no one responds. He's our God, and He has what we need, but He is waiting for us to come to Him as we should. Do it today. And never forget: there is an inseparable link between your desire and your destiny.

Chapter 6

WHY TWENTY-FIRST CENTURY CHRISTIANS DON'T PRAY

But if from thence thou shalt seek the Lord thy God, thou shalt find him, if thou seek him with all thy heart and with all thy soul.

Deuteronomy 4:29

Nothing has been done in the earth that hasn't come through prayer, nothing supernatural has ever been accomplished without being preceded by prayer, and there has never been a revival or a move of God that wasn't birthed through prayer. The Bible declares this truth in simplicity:

Ye have not, because ye ask not.

James 4:2

We have seen in previous chapters the fact that prayer is our life force, the secret of tapping into the divine. So why are people not praying more today, in the twenty-first century?

There are some rather obvious reasons, it seems to me, why people no longer pray. We have already looked at some of them in passing, but let us now take a closer look at several reasons for this most serious failure of ours.

As we discuss reasons that people no longer pray, I encourage you to search your own heart. When I am preparing to preach any message, part of what I do is search my own heart to see if I fall short in regard to the subject I'm about to preach. Wouldn't it be terrible to preach something to others and then fail to live up to it myself? I love to be challenged in this way. Even when I hear others preaching, I love it when their message gets down deep into my soul and shines its searchlight on my personal life. I'm not interested in having my ears tickled. I want to get ready for revival.

Here are a few of the key reasons I believe modern Americans are failing in the important responsibility of prayer.

BECAUSE THEY DON'T KNOW HOW TO PRAY

Many Christians are convinced that they just don't know how to pray. Everything about our modern world is so technical and so well-defined and documented that they expect to have a better manual on correct prayer procedures any day now. But the truth is that there is no one "correct" way to pray.

It's not wrong to read good books on prayer or listen to good sermons on prayer, but don't think that anyone can teach you the way you should pray personally. That's between you and God. You will develop it by doing it.

Prayer Is Personal—Between You and God:

When people ask me how to pray, I tell them that they can learn just by doing it. Prayer is something that no one can really teach you to do and do well. Start praying, and be led by the Spirit.

Why is this true? It's because prayer is such a personal thing between you and God. It would be wrong for you to simply imitate the way others pray. You have to learn your own way of praying.

No one had to teach me how to talk with my husband. Because we loved each other, we just did it. And we learned by doing.

One thing I know: the more you pray, the more you will want to pray, and the less you pray, the less you will want to pray. Get started, and you will improve.

As we noted in an earlier chapter, Jesus taught us a few basic guidelines about prayer in the model prayer we call The Lord's Prayer. There He taught us the importance of including much praise and worship in our prayers. He taught us to first be concerned about the larger picture, His kingdom and His will for the earth, and to leave our personal concerns for later. And there are a few other important lessons to be learned from that prayer.

Prayer Must Be a Two-Way Street:

The reason some people can't seem to pray very long is that they're doing all the talking. Prayer must be a two-way street. You have to talk to God, but then you have to listen to what He says to you in return. When you're doing all the talking, you're missing out on the most important half of your prayer life. Give God a chance to talk to your spirit.

Prayer Must Be from the Heart:

There is another thing that the Scriptures make very clear about prayer: it must be from the heart. God is not interested in phony conversations with anyone. And, believe me, He knows when they're phony. We'll develop this thought more fully in the final section of this chapter.

BECAUSE THEY'RE NOT GETTING ANSWERS TO PRAYERS ALREADY PRAYED

Another reason people are not praying is that they've not been getting answers to the prayers they've already prayed. If people could just ask God for anything they wanted and get it, they would be lining up at our church doors waiting for prayer time to begin. Why are good people praying what seem like good prayers, and still they're not answered? There are a number of reasons this might be true.

We're Very Impatient People:

One of the reasons our prayers are not answered is that we're very impatient people. We live in a world of convenience and comfort, and if God doesn't answer as quickly as we think He should, we resort to other means. We're not about to wait around for Him.

We Ask for Things That Are Not Good for Us:

God has promised us:

No good thing will he withhold from them that walk uprightly.

Psalm 84:11

If, then, I ask for something, and I don't receive it, it must mean that God knows that the thing I have asked Him for is not good for me. In that case, I should be thankful that He withholds it.

Our Timing Is Sometimes Off:

Another reason my prayers may be delayed or denied is that the timing is not right. God knows so much better than I do when the precise moment to answer my prayers has come, and, as we're all fond of saying, "He's never late."

Prayer Demands Perseverance:

Another reason we may not be getting answers to our prayers is that prayer demands a certain perseverance, as if to prove to God that we're serious and trust Him. When we pray, we're to *"ask."* If the answer doesn't come immediately, we're to *"seek."* If the answer still doesn't come, we're to *"knock"* (Matthew 7:7-8). This shows us the element of persistence that is needed for successful prayer. We must be determined not to let go until the answer comes. When the perseverance is there, we can also expect the answer to our prayers.

We Often Pray Very Selfish Prayers:

If your prayer life is being conducted selfishly, you're missing out on a great deal. It is still a greater blessing to give than it is to receive. Your prayer life should be centered around God's Kingdom, His will for you and others, His church and where it's going these days. Learn to pray His heart. His Word promises:

And this is the confidence that we have in him, that, if we ask any thing according to his will, he heareth us. And if we know that he hear us, whatsoever we ask, we know that we have the petitions that we desired of him.

1 John 5:14-15

There is no biblical promise that, when we have prayed according to our own will, we can be confident of receiving an answer from God. Some people have been praying for years now for a better house, and they don't understand why God's not answering that prayer. That really bothers me. God wants you to have a good house, but that's not a subject worthy of your prayer focus. Get your mind onto more important things, and your prayer life will become fruitful.

Many times we don't even have to pray for material things. God just sends them our way.

Many times we don't even have to pray for material things. God just sends them our way. If we pray that His will be done on the earth and that His kingdom come, and we're doing all that we know to do to bring that about, He'll make things happen for us. His promise is clear:

Seek ye first the kingdom of God, and his righteousness; and all these things shall be added unto you.

Matthew 6:33

Learning to pray unselfishly will bring many new and wonderful benefits to your life.

Some Prayers Go Awry:

Not only do we pray selfish prayers and pray for things that are not good for us. Sometimes our prayers seem to go awry. We *"ask amiss."* When this happens, God's response (or lack of response) is predictable. He said:

> *Ye ask, and receive not, because ye ask amiss, that ye may consume it upon your lusts.*
>
> James 4:3

A bigger car, a bigger house, a raise, a better job ... these are not wrong desires necessarily, but it's wrong that they are allowed to consume so much of our time and attention—at the expense of far more important matters. "Gimme, gimme, gimme" is a very childish approach to prayer. It may be normal for children to have childish desires, but it's not normal for those who are supposed to be mature believers in Christ. Children think of no one but themselves, but grown-ups should know better.

The Importance of Praying According to God's Will:

According to 1 John 5:14, we can be confident that God hears what we say to Him in prayer only when we pray *"according to His will."* When we're off praying our own thing, asking for what we want and not what He wants, asking for things that we may even know are not good for us, God doesn't even listen.

We do the same thing with our children. When they reach driving age, if they say to us, "Mama, I want a new Mercedes," our response is swift and decisive: "Hush up with that foolish-ness." And I'm afraid that's what God is forced to say to many Christians when they pray their foolishness.

Verse fifteen of that chapter shows us how effective prayer can be in the life of the believer. Again, it says: *"And if we know that he hear us, whatsoever we ask, we know that we have the petitions that we desired of him."* Many other Bible passages confirm this truth:

The effectual fervent prayer of a righteous man availeth much.

James 5:16

And all things, whatsoever ye shall ask in prayer, believing, ye shall receive.

Matthew 21:22

He will regard the prayer of the destitute, and not despise their prayer.

Psalm 102:17

Still, despite all of these promises (and there are many more), God cannot answer us when we *"ask amiss."* If what we ask for is for our own lust and hurt, what father could answer a prayer like that?

In the prayer of Jesus in Gethsemane, we have a perfect example of how we can pray in the will of God. Jesus was enjoying life and had every reason to live. He was not thrilled with the idea of giving His life on Calvary. Plus, what the Father was asking Him to do (take upon himself the sins of the whole world) was so terrible that He felt He simply could not bear it. He cried out to the Father:

O my Father, if it be possible, let this cup pass from me.

Matthew 26:39

What was set before Jesus was so terrible to behold that His perspiration began to come as great drops of blood. Several times, He asked the Father if there might not be some other way to save mankind.

Then suddenly something changed. As Jesus looked into the cup held out to Him by the Father, He saw something. Personally, I've always believed that He saw people and their need for His sacrifice. He saw men and women locked in prisons with no hope for the future. He saw men and women with needles stuck in their veins, filling themselves with damaging drugs. He saw women selling their bodies in the streets of the cities of the world. When He saw all of that, His prayer changed, and He became willing to do whatever was necessary to save mankind. He prayed:

Nevertheless not as I will, but as thou wilt.

Matthew 26:39

Jesus was willing to drink that bitter cup so that those in prison could become preachers of the gospel, so that those shooting up drugs could become youth leaders, and so that those who once prostituted themselves on the streets could become Sunday school teachers. And so His mind was made up, and He was ready for the cross and ready for death. He was ready because He now understood the will of the Father, to bring redemption to all mankind. How could He oppose such a great purpose?

When your prayer changes from one that seeks only your own good to one that seeks the good of God's kingdom and the people around you, then all of heaven will suddenly stand at attention, and you will get results you have only dreamed of until now.

If your prayers are not being answered, check to see if one of these might be the reason.

BECAUSE THEIR PRIORITIES ARE ALL "MESSED UP"

Another reason people don't pray today is because their priorities are all "messed up." This word *priority* means "precedence, especially established by order of importance or urgency."

A priority indicates the importance you place on something. Most Americans think first about their job and the income it provides for them. Next, they think about their family, about their house and car (and maybe the boat in the garage). Unfortunately, God is way down on their list of priorities, and so it's no wonder they don't have time to pray. Other things are more important to them.

To many people, mowing the grass is more important than attending a prayer meeting. If it's not the grass, then they have to clean out the garage, or they can always find a thousand other things they've been wanting to do for a long time. But what about God?

Make an Appointment with God:

Isn't it time that we made an appointment with God. These days, it seems that we have appointments for everyone and everything else in life except Him. Married couples even make an appointment (better known as a date) with each other in order to be able to spend meaningful time together.

If you'll make an appointment with God, I guarantee that He'll show up and be on time. Will you?

We have a common misconception because we talk about "waiting on God." That doesn't mean that He's not there. In reality, we're not waiting on Him; He's waiting on us.

Proper priorities demand that we take time to be alone with God. If those of us who are married don't spend time alone with our spouse, we won't make it as a couple. Time alone should be what we crave.

If you'll make an appointment with God, I guarantee that He'll show up and be on time. Will you?

Women, there should be times when you decide to leave the dirty dishes in the sink or the clothes waiting to be folded and go spend some meaningful time with your spouse. And the same is true about God. If you've never had a spontaneous experience like that, then your spiritual life is in danger.

Let other things go for the moment. There will be time for them later. Take care of the more important things in life. God wants to talk to you. Give Him the time He deserves.

How precious it should be to us that the God of the universe would say to us, "Come aside. I want to talk to you." Don't ever take that lightly.

He spoke and the worlds were formed, and yet He would stoop down to say to me, "Darlene, I want to talk to you." What a privilege! Would I ever dare to say that I was too busy? Would

I object, saying that I had dishes to do or supper to cook? I would never do that.

If the President would call your house some day and ask to speak with you, would it even occur to you to say that you were too busy? I don't think so. What about God? Is He not much more important than any president?

We're talking about God. He's the one who gives us breath to exist. He spoke to us through His servants, the early apostles, and said:

Let us therefore come boldly unto the throne of grace, that we may obtain mercy, and find grace to help in time of need.

Hebrews 4:16

What am I waiting for? Mowing your lawn regularly is important, but prayer is much more important. Caring for your plants is important, but prayer is much more important. Improving your house is important, but prayer is much more important.

Even Ministers Sometimes Need to Check Their Priorities:

Even ministers need to get their priorities straight. At one point, God said to me, "Preach on prayer until I tell you to quit." That let me know that many people were not praying as they should, and even though there are more popular subjects to be preached, I obeyed Him.

If we want people to be saved in our churches, we need a life of prayer. Prayer is what will draw them to the church, and prayer is what will draw them to the altar. Having a great choir is never enough.

We can only preach under the anointing when we've prayed, and we surely ought to know by now that it's the anointing of the Spirit that destroys yokes, opens prison doors, and binds up broken hearts. God may let us get by a few times without praying, but before long a testimony we have given with power many times before may begin to sound dull and lifeless and no longer have the same effect.

When the anointing is present, men and women who are bound in the prisons of drugs, alcohol, and perversion will be set free. Prayer is the key to their freedom and restoration.

What Does Our Choice of Priorities Signal to God?

We know all of this, and yet we allow many things, too many things, to take priority over God. How does that sound to Him? I'm afraid it signals to Him that we no longer love Him as much as we used to.

CNN interviewed a young woman who had married a feeble old millionaire. When he died, not long afterward, she inherited eighty million dollars from his estate. She insisted that they had been "in love." When pressed further, she admitted that he had gone to bed at six each evening, and then she had gone out with friends and done her own thing. To most observers, that didn't sound much like love.

How foolish it must sound to God when we publicly profess to love Him and have Him as Lord of our lives and then fail to give Him the time He deserves. He said:

Not every one that saith unto me, Lord, Lord, shall enter into the kingdom of heaven; but he that doeth the will of my Father which is in heaven.

Matthew 7:21

121

It gets worse. The people in question say to Him that they have prophesied in His name, cast out devils, and done many other wonderful works. Still, He says to them these chilling words:

I never knew you: depart from me, ye that work iniquity.

Matthew 7:23

This word *iniquity* means lawlessness, doing your own thing. So I can be healing the sick and casting out the devils, and still be doing it for my own glory, not God's.

Some time ago, I saw a film done about a young man who'd had a near-death experience. Doctors had pronounced him clinically dead, and yet he had somehow survived. He said that during the time he was dead, he stood before a Being who was sheathed in such brightness that he was unable to look upon Him. The Being asked, "What have you done with your life?" And the young man began to relate what he had done thus far. He sensed that the Being knew everything and that it would be useless to lie to Him.

"You did all of that for you," the Being said. "What did you do for Me?" And the man was left speechless. Grateful for having been given a second chance at life, he was now determined to do better.

Removing Money from the Equation:

I'm afraid that many preachers are preaching for their own ulterior motives, and many gospel singers are singing for the same reason. If you took money and fame out of the equation, there would probably be a mass exodus from the ministry. How many preachers would continue preaching if it was ruled that they could receive no money for it?

Many would literally run from the stage. "Forget that bunch," they might say. "Let them all go to hell! I'm not messing with them anymore." It would happen because so many have their priorities all "messed up."

In the twenty-first century, we're much too enthralled with material things and far less enthralled with the one who created all of those things and entrusted them to our keeping. We're too busy enjoying life to think about the one who gives life and gives it more abundantly. But life is not about how many things you can collect. Hold lightly to the things entrusted to you, but cling to the God who has given them.

I would gladly exchange my house and car, if it were necessary, for the continuing privilege of being in the Lord's presence. He is my life, and the closer I get to Him the less things mean to me. We don't need big houses; we need more of God. Just one touch from Him, just one glimpse, is more important than anything and everything I have ever possessed. Let's get our priorities straight!

How Did Our Priorities Get So "Messed Up"?

How did our priorities get so "messed up"? We're so attached to the things of this world. Yet these things will all fade away in time and, therefore, amount to very little. Of them, the Bible says, *"Which all are to perish with the using"* (Colossians 2:22). We're so intent on chasing the pleasures of this world, and yet we have not given God His rightful place. Just think about the amount of time we have wasted on frivolous things.

123

It's wonderful to have family time, and I'm surely not against that, but why can't God then have His fair share of our time too? How many times have we stood in line for an hour at an amusement park in order to take a thirty-second ride, and we didn't think anything about it? How many times have we waited an hour or more just to eat at some good restaurant? That's not necessarily bad, but why can't God get His turn with our attentions?

I'm afraid that it's because we've left our *"first love."*

BECAUSE THEY'VE LEFT THEIR "FIRST LOVE"

In Revelation 2, Jesus spoke through John to the church at Ephesus. He commended them for the good things they were doing, but He went on to say that He had something against them. They had left their *"first love"* (Revelation 2:4). I used to preach that this only meant that they had stopped experiencing joy in attending church services, singing in the church choir, and hearing the preaching of the Word of God. But one day God showed me that it meant much more. Let's take a closer look at exactly what Jesus said to the church at Ephesus:

Unto the angel of the church of Ephesus write; These things saith he that holdeth the seven stars in his right hand, who walketh in the midst of the seven golden candlesticks; I know thy works, and thy labour, and thy patience, and how thou canst not bear them which are evil: and thou hast tried them which say they are apostles, and are not, and hast found them liars: and hast borne, and hast patience, and for my name's sake hast laboured, and hast not fainted. Nevertheless I have somewhat against thee, because thou hast left thy first love. Remember therefore from whence thou art fallen, and repent, and do the first works; or else I will come unto thee quickly, and will remove thy candlestick out of his place, except thou repent.

Revelation 2:1-5

God showed it to me this way: Lawrence Bishop was my first love and the only man I ever said, "I love you" to. Lawrence has richly blessed my life and has given me many wonderful things. No woman could ask for more.

Spending More Time with Created Things Than with the Creator:

But what would happen if I, for some reason, started spending more time with the things Lawrence has given me and neglected to spend time with the person himself? That would be a tragic mistake, wouldn't it?

That's what happened at Ephesus. The people were doing a great work *for* God, but they were not doing enough *with* God. That would be like me staying away from home for long periods of time and saying to Lawrence, "I still love you, but I'm too busy to spend time with you anymore. Please keep working and supplying my needs, but in the meantime, I'll be off at such-and-such vacation resort doing my own thing. It would be better if you don't bother me because I have a lot going on right now." That wouldn't be much of a relationship, would it?

In the same way, I need to spend time with God. It's not enough that I travel all over the world *for* Him, preaching five to seven times a week and spending twenty to thirty hours a week studying the Scriptures in preparation for that ministry. If I haven't spent quality time with God, then I'm neglecting my *"first love."*

You can be going all the right places and doing all of the right things and still miss it. There must be a time when we come apart, go into some secret place, and say to the Lord, "There, Lord. Now it's just You and me."

Together in the Secret Place:

How would it seem to a person to whom you were engaged to be married if you said, "Well, this has been lovely. I'll see you again for a few minutes a week from now at this same time." What an insult! Would we ever consider spending only an hour and a half a week with someone we love? And yet, although we're part of the bride of Christ, we do that to Him far too often.

If a woman loves a man and wants to be part of his life, she makes sure that he knows where she is and what she's doing at all times. She makes sure that they have time to be together and get to know each other intimately.

Something Against Us:

We prefer to look at the first part of Jesus' comments to the first-century church at Ephesus, for we love commendations. But He didn't stop there. He went on to say, *"Nevertheless, I have something against you."* And that something was that they had left Him out of too many things. They were not developing enough intimacy with Him.

When I'm on the road, there's always someone from our church accompanying me. But although I love their company, there come moments when I need some time alone with God, and I ask them to excuse themselves. The moment they close that hotel door, the presence of God floods the room, and although I may be a little hoarse from preaching, in those moments I sing to Jesus.

When was the last time you sang a song to the Lord?

When was the last time you sang a song to the Lord? Oh, I know that you join in the congregational singing from time to time, but do you ever just sing to Him on your own, when no one else is listening? It doesn't matter if you can sing well or not. When you sing to Him, it sounds good to Him, and that's all that matters.

How long has it been? How long has it been since you said to the Lord, "I want to just sit here in Your presence and meditate on Your goodness. I just want to thank You, Lord, for everything You've done for me. You're such a good God. I thank You because of who and what You are to me."

What Does It Mean?

When we say that a person has lost their *"first love,"* it doesn't mean that they no longer love anything about God. It's possible to love the trappings of Christianity and still not love the Christ of Christianity. It's possible to get so caught up in doing His work that we forget the Man behind the works.

The people of the church at Ephesus had labored hard. They hated sin and compromise. They didn't faint when they were persecuted. They had one flaw, but it was a serious one—a deadly one. They had begun to leave God out of the equation. Far too many people are so busy doing the work of God that they forget the God of the work.

We can give, we can love others, and we can hate sin, but if our heart isn't drawn to the presence of God, we simply don't love Him as we used to. There's no other way to explain it.

If you don't love being around a person it means that you don't love that person. What else can it mean? When you would rather be doing something else than staying in the presence of God, that's proof enough that you no longer love Him in the same way.

He created you to have fellowship with Him, but He can't force you to love Him. Jesus died for you because He wanted to be one with you, and now here you are off doing your own thing, rarely talking to Him, rarely consulting Him on the serious issues of your life, and rarely including Him in the activities you plan. If He were number one in your life, you wouldn't make a single decision or take a single step without including Him.

Can Children Live without their Father?

We're God's children, and He's our Father, but if our lives reflect prayerlessness, that indicates to Him that we have become independent of Him and no longer need Him. Can this be right?

Any child needs its father. A child is dependant upon its father for every need and every decision. Children can't make decisions, and we're children. We desperately need our heavenly Father. Why don't we recognize that fact?

With the advance of modern psychology, we're discovering that the reason many people seem to have very warped personalities these days is that they lacked the meaningful participation of a father in their growing-up years. Such people have great difficulty understanding the place of God in their lives. They need to learn all over again what it means to have a Father.

Remaining Childlike:

Jesus taught us that we should become more childlike:

Verily I say unto you, Except ye be converted, and become as little children, ye shall not enter into the kingdom of heaven. Whosoever therefore shall humble himself as this little child, the same is greatest in the kingdom of heaven.

Matthew 18:3-4

In our churches these days, we often talk of the need to be born again, but once that is accomplished, we usually think that we're suddenly all grown up and can do things on our own. That's simply not the case.

On another occasion, Jesus again showed His disciples the importance of being childlike:

And they brought young children to him, that he should touch them: and his disciples rebuked those that brought them. But when Jesus saw it, he was much displeased, and said unto them, Suffer the little children to come unto me, and forbid them not: for of such is the kingdom of God. Verily I say unto you, Whosoever shall not receive the kingdom of God as a little child, he shall not enter therein. And he took them up in his arms, put his hands upon them, and blessed them.

Mark 10:13-16

God's kingdom is made up of His children, and His children depend on Him for everything. That requires that we form a more loving and communicative bond with Him.

Prepare for the Future:

We are in the process of being formed into the bride of Christ, and He will one day be joined to us in marriage, so that we can spend eternity with Him. But how can we hope to achieve that coveted position if we don't take time now to get to know Him better, to become intimate with Him?

And how can we expect to escape the difficult times that will come upon the earth if we have neglected to build our relationship with God through prayer now? The times that are ahead will be as none other:

This know also, that in the last days perilous times shall come.

2 Timothy 3:1

If we are forced to face such times without knowing well the voice of God, we will surely find ourselves in serious trouble. Listen to Him more now, so that you can recognize His voice later.

Learn to Know His Voice:

How is it that we know the voice of our spouse, the voice of our children, and the voice of our friends, and yet we don't know the voice of God? We know the voice of popular singers, media personalities, and politicians, and yet we don't know the voice of God.

We know the popular voices of our day because that's what we listen to on a regular basis. We don't know God's voice because we don't listen to Him nearly enough.

This is serious. We are constantly under attack from hell, and we're being tempted and tried every day. Yet we go for weeks without ever calling on the name of the Lord, who is our strength. If we know that *"prayer ... availeth much,"* why is it that we don't pray more? When we know God's promises that *"all things whatsoever we ask in prayer believing, we shall receive"* and that *"we have this confidence that if we ask anything that it shall be done,"* why don't we pray more?

Why don't we pray? Because we have not known how, because we have not been getting answer to prayers already prayed, and because our priorities have been all "messed up." But the worst indictment against us is that we don't pray because we've left our "first love." That means that the passion has gone out of the marriage, the intensity of our spiritual desire has diminished.

Although the Scriptures do not teach us techniques of prayer, they do teach us the importance of the intensity of our prayers. James, for instance wrote:

> *The effectual fervent prayer of a righteous man availeth much.*
>
> James 5:16

There is a certain type of prayer that God says is effective. It's not a prayer of particular words; it's a prayer of particular intensity, a *"fervent prayer."*

According to *Webster's Dictionary* this word *effectual* means "producing or able to produce a desired effect." An effectual prayer is one that affects its object. According to *Strong's*, *fervent* here means "very hot, glowing; exhibiting or marked by great intensity of feeling; zealous." That's the kind of prayers that produce the desired result. Alas, when we have lost our "first love," this type of prayer becomes difficult or impossible.

Before we move on and take a look at the remedy for having lost one's *"first love,"* there is one more reason we might mention quickly—people in the twenty-first century don't pray. They know what's right and good, but they are procrastinators.

THEY PUT OFF THE NEED TO DEVELOP A PRAYER LIFE

When we're young, we always think that we'll have plenty of time for God in the future. At the moment, we're full of vim and vigor, and there are so many things we need to experience in life. Later we plan to give God the time we know He deserves.

But, for some odd reason, that time for developing a prayer life never seems to come. The reason is that as we age, nothing changes.

When you reach fifty, you feel as young as ever, and you still don't want life to pass you by. So you postpone your date with God for another decade or so. And another. And another.

This same pattern often continues, until one day people lie dying in some hospital bed. Only then do they wake up and realize that they have allowed life's most important things to pass them by, without laying hold of them. They are saddened. But, of course, it's too late. Please don't be one of those people.

THE REMEDY FOR HAVING FORSAKEN OUR "FIRST LOVE"

If you have left your *"first love,"* as often happens, what's the remedy for it? Jesus went on to say to the Ephesian church:

> *Remember therefore from whence thou art fallen, and repent, and do the first works; or else I will come unto thee quickly, and will remove thy candlestick out of his place, except thou repent.*

Revelation 2:5

"Repent and do the first works." There is no other remedy. You must return to your first love. You must experience a revival of passion in your Christian experience and learn again to pray those white-hot prayers you used to pray, the ones that you sensed penetrated space and landed directly at God's throne. Those prayers got answers, and it can happen again.

Where Do You Stand?'

Where do you stand? If God were to judge your prayer life today, would you receive a passing grade? Does He have something against you? Are your priorities right? Is He your first responder in every situation of life?

He very much wants to manifest His glory in your life and to give you miracles on a daily basis. But that can't happen until you recognize Him as your source and seek Him in all things, until He can see that you're really in love with Him and want His presence with you.

Are We Ready?

Are we ready to make God's house a house of prayer again, as He intended?

Mine house shall be called an house of prayer for all people.

Isaiah 56:7

Are we ready to be the praying person God has called us to be? If so, we must humble ourselves before Him today. Bow in His presence, hungry for more of Him. Let Him know how very much you need Him, and ask Him to forgive you for having been too busy doing things that won't matter much in the light of eternity. Then take time to praise Him.

When was the last time you spent moments before Him on your knees? Do it today. Nothing could be more important. Thank Him. Tell Him how much you value your relationship with Him. Tell Him how much you value His presence in your life.

Ask the Lord to restore your *"first love"* to you, to put within you once again a burning desire for time in prayer, time in His Word, and time in His church. Let Him know that you want Him more than anything else in life.

Give Him all of your hopes and dreams and trust Him to guide you into His very best for your life in the days ahead. Give Him everything, and thus make Him the center of your affections.

Tell Him that you just can't live without Him, that you need Him more than the air you breathe and more than the song you sing. Lean back and rest in His warm embrace. Don't be in a hurry to leave that secret place where the two of you meet.

Linger in His presence. That's the only remedy for prayerlessness. Tell Him today, "Lord, forgive us for our prayerlessness." And never forget: there is an inseparable link between your desire and your destiny.

Chapter 7

THE LOSS OF DESIRE AND THE RESULTANT DISOBEDIENCE

Wherefore seeing we also are compassed about with so great a cloud of witnesses, let us lay aside every weight, and the sin which doth so easily beset us, and let us run with patience the race that is set before us

Hebrews 12:1

According to *Strong's*, this word *weight* means "a hindrance or burden." It's not necessarily something evil in itself, but it does evil by dulling your conscience and choking out the spirit of prayer in your life. A weight is anything that pulls you down and makes living for God more difficult for you.

When the Spirit of God begins to reveal to you the weights in your life, He'll also give you the power to lay them aside. Then it's up to you. Anything that hinders the will of God in your life should be forsaken if you want to make spiritual progress. And that's true whether you consider a thing to be sin or not. Any weight, if it is not quickly cast off, will hold you down.

WRITTEN TO SINNERS OR TO SAINTS?

This passage of Scripture was clearly written to Christians, not sinners. To many sinners, the concept of sin has very little meaning. Those who are not believers in Christ rarely, if ever, consider their actions to be sin. For them, what they're doing is normal behavior. They're just doing what comes naturally, what's in their nature to do. Sin is a Christian concept and can be understood only by those who long to do God's will and live a life pleasing to Him.

A sinner may be able to stop some offensive behavior, but he can never stop being a sinner. That's what he is. Turning over a new leaf will not save him. By nature, he's a sinner, and unless God changes him, he'll always remain a sinner.

The concept of sin is very meaningful to those who know God. If a sinner lays aside weights in his life, others replace them. He's still on his way to hell. Only a believer in Christ can successfully lay aside weights and expect his or her life to change dramatically. So start laying aside the weights you discover, and don't stop until every weight has been dealt with.

Sin has a way of wrapping itself around you, and if its hold is not quickly broken, it will pull you down and smother you in the process. Sin will always take you further than you wanted to go and keep you longer then you wanted to stay.

Most of us have one particular area of vulnerability, one area of special weakness, and this is what the Scriptures mean by *"the sin which doth so easily beset us."* You may not be tempted by the things that tempt others, but something draws you aside. If you follow it, it will lead you into other sins as well.

YOUR CURRENT STRUGGLE IS NOTHING NEW

For most of us, the struggle we're currently involved in is nothing new. It's the same old thing we've been struggling with for years. When we're saved, our "old man" dies, but he constantly struggles to rise again and take control of our lives.

Those who had an appetite for drugs or alcohol before they were saved often have recurring battles with the same temptations afterwards. If, at some point, they succumb to sin and backslide, they usually go right back to the same thing they were delivered from.

The same is true for illicit sex and other fleshly pursuits. Therefore, our victory over the particular sin that torments us must be a recurring one.

Unfortunately, hell knows exactly what your particular weakness is. That's where you'll be tested over and over again, and you'll be tested in ways that others can only imagine. Because others might never think of succumbing to that particular temptation, Satan doesn't even bother tempting them in that way.

DISTRACTIONS CAN BE FATAL

This word *beset*, according to *Strong's* is what happens to a competitor getting ready for a race, when he's suddenly distracted by somebody or something in his surroundings. As a consequence, what he sees hinders him from concentrating on the task at hand, his important race. That can be fatal, and it happens very easily as the text shows us.

The presence of any weight in your life changes your focus. Instead of focusing on God, you begin to focus on the things and the people around you. Thus, any weight becomes a hindrance. It could cause you to be sidelined from the race, to fall behind, or even to be forcibly removed from the race.

The presence of any weight in your life changes your focus.

When a serious runner is standing on his mark at a starting line, he knows that it's not the time to be looking around. He has one thing on his mind. He has a race to run. Anything that he allows to distract him will only hinder his prospects for victory. With those who are not as serious, such distractions can easily occur.

As we have noted, when people are newly saved, they have a joy that seems to know no bounds. They can hardly talk without tears coming to their eyes. They love to read the Word of God and listen to good teaching—wherever they can find it. They love to go to church, and those moments in which they can interact with other Christians brings great joy to their lives.

But just let the weights begin to come, and soon they dread going to church and meeting other people. Instead of bringing them joy, it now becomes a chore for them. They say a prayer now and then to ease their conscience, but they dread the idea of a real prayer time. They put their Bible on the shelf when they get home each Sunday and rarely pick it up through the rest of the week. No wonder their old habits begin to surface!

Often nobody else knows what's happening to people like this. In every other way, they seem normal. They're still going through the motions of being a good Christian, but their heart is just not in it.

DEALING WITH YOUR MIRY PLACES

The prophet Ezekiel had a vision of a place that badly needed watering, and then he saw rivers flowing toward it. He said:

And it shall come to pass, that every thing that liveth, whithersoever the rivers shall come, shall live.

Ezekiel 47:9

That's a picture of the abundant life the Lord offers us. But not every place benefited. Ezekiel went on to say:

But the miry places thereof and the marshes thereof shall not be healed.

Ezekiel 47:11

This is phenomenal! The vision Ezekiel received that day depicts great revival, the flowing of rivers of life into a dry situation, and the bringing of new and abundant life to everything it touched. But, for some reason, some places were left untouched by it all. Why would that be?

"Miry places" and *"marshes"* are places that already have some water, but that water is not fresh. It gets trapped in there, and then it stagnates. Thus it is that, right there in the midst of the flow of the river of God, there are untouched and unchanged places. While everyone around them is being changed, they remain much as they were before.

Swampy, or *"miry"* places represent self-centeredness, an inward focus. Water comes in, but then it's trapped and, because it has no outlet, it stagnates.

Some people are like that. They're so self-centered, so inwardly focused, that nothing else matters to them. They demand that others let them have what they want and let them do what they want. And as difficult as it seems, as God is moving around them, they remain unmoved by it. Other people are being healed on every side of them, and yet they remain crippled and in need. Nothing seems to reach them.

Oh, they go to church, but when they leave, they leave the same as they were when they arrived. In the services, hell can be preached so well that people around them feel its flames, but they feel nothing. Heaven can be declared in such a sweet way that others almost feel as if they're already there. Yet these people remain unmoved. How terrible!

David knew what it was to be trapped in *"miry clay,"* but he came forth:

He brought me up also out of an horrible pit, out of the miry clay, and set my feet upon a rock, and established my goings.

Psalm 40:2

Let God bring you out today and then get quickly into the flow of His river. Refuse to stay in your swamp any longer.

It's not uncommon for men and women to preach things from the pulpit and not be able to live them on a day-to-day basis because of *"miry places"* that exist in their personal lives. They say all the right things and do the right things in public, but they have areas that they can't seem to get control of, temptations they can't seem to get victory over. If left unchecked, this ultimately destroys them and their ministry.

SOLOMON'S MIRY PLACES

There are some striking biblical examples of this phenomenon. Solomon, for instance, was David's favorite son, and he was chosen by God to be the heir to his father's throne. As we noted in an earlier chapter, Solomon had a supernatural visitation from God in which God offered him anything he wanted, and as a result, he became the wisest man who ever lived.

David had longed to build a suitable house for God in Jerusalem, but because he was a man of war, God reserved that privilege for Solomon. David left his son extensive plans and materials that he had accumulated for the project. In the end, Solomon's kingdom went far beyond his fathers, and the riches and might of the two men could hardly be compared.

And yet there were serious flaws in Solomon and in his reign over Israel:

And Solomon loved the Lord, walking in the statutes of David his father: only he sacrificed and burnt incense in the high places.

1 Kings 3:3

Isn't that amazing? Solomon loved God, and yet he fell short in this way. There's more:

It came to pass, when Solomon was old, that his wives turned away his heart after other gods: and his heart was not perfect with the Lord his God, as was the heart of David his father.

1 Kings 11:4

This was not some mild flirtation with other gods. This was a serious departure from truth and right. The story continues:

For Solomon went after Ashtoreth the goddess of the Zidonians, and after Milcom the abomination of the Ammonites. And Solomon did evil in the sight of the Lord, and went not fully after the Lord, as did David his father. Then did Solomon build an high place for Chemosh, the abomination of Moab, in the hill that is before Jerusalem, and for Molech, the abomination of the children of Ammon. And likewise did he for all his strange wives, which burnt incense and sacrificed unto their gods.

1 Kings 11:5-8

To those of us who understand the grandeur of Solomon's reign, this seems inconceivable, and yet it happened.

Of course, Solomon's backsliding didn't happen overnight. It began as one weight, one distraction, something that took his attention away from God. It grew in intensity from there, and the result was this tragedy of idol worship and the loss of God's favor that followed it.

God was understandably angry with Solomon. He had entrusted much into his hands, and Solomon had not handled it well:

And the Lord was angry with Solomon, because his heart was turned from the Lord God of Israel, which had appeared unto him twice, and had commanded him concerning this thing, that he should not go after other gods: but he kept not that which the Lord commanded. Wherefore the Lord said unto Solomon, Forasmuch as this is done of thee, and thou hast not kept my covenant and my statutes, which I have commanded thee, I will surely rend the kingdom from thee, and will give it to thy servant. Notwithstanding in thy days I will not do it for David thy father's sake: but I will rend it out of the hand of thy son. Howbeit I will not rend away all the kingdom; but will give one tribe to thy son for David my servant's sake, and for Jerusalem's sake which I have chosen.

1 Kings 11:9-13

What finally seems to have gotten Solomon's attention was the fact that the Lord stirred up an enemy against him:

And the Lord stirred up an adversary against Solomon, Hadad the Edomite: he was of the kings seed in Edom.

1 Kings 11:14

How sad it is that God had to resort to such lengths to get Solomon's attention! For an extended period of time King Solomon had enjoyed a blessed peace with his neighbors roundabout. He had marveled at this:

But now the Lord my God hath given me rest on every side, so that there is neither adversary nor evil occurrent.

1 Kings 5:4

But that was then, and this was now. Then he had been experiencing an unusual period of peace with his neighbors, but now he was suddenly faced with an angry enemy.

As long as Solomon was doing the right thing, God made his enemies to be at peace with him, but when he lost his spiritual focus, trouble came. How was it that a man who was so blessed by God was preparing places of idol worship for others? This could not be permitted.

143

It should shake us to the core to realize that a man like Solomon who knew so much and had so much at his disposal could be sidetracked in this way. If this could happen to the wisest man who ever lived, how much more could it happen to any one of us?

Here was a man who was deeply involved in the work of the Lord and who was chosen to lead others, and yet his own life was now out of control. We've all seen it happen in our lifetime. Men who were revered as God's anointed servants suddenly became headlines for CNN and our local evening newscasts, where they were portrayed as clowns. It happened because they had some *"miry place"* in their lives that had not been touched by the river of life.

Sin, the Bible assures us, must be confessed and forsaken. If this is not done, it *"will surely find you out"* (Numbers 32:23).

ELIASHIB'S MIRY PLACES

As we noted earlier, Nehemiah, an exile from Jerusalem, was doing well in Persia, when God raised him up and sent him back to rebuild the Holy City. Two men who heard about this desire vowed to stop him. They were Sanballat and Tobiah. At first, these two men tried to laugh Nehemiah and his people to scorn:

> *But it came to pass, that when Sanballat heard that we builded the wall, he was wroth, and took great indignation, and mocked the Jews.*
>
> Nehemiah 4:1

Tobiah was even more vehement in his disdain for the builders:

Now Tobiah the Ammonite was by him, and he said, Even that which they build, if a fox go up, he shall even break down their stone wall.

Nehemiah 4:3

This is significant because Tobiah was an Ammonite. The Ammonites and the Moabites were heathen people who hated the God of Israel. They were the same people who had tried to get a prophet named Balaam to curse the children of Israel as they were coming through their land. God had declared of them:

An Ammonite or Moabite shall not enter into the congregation of the Lord; even to their tenth generation shall they not enter into the congregation of the Lord for ever.

Deuteronomy 23:3

That's how fierce the enmity was between these people and the servants of God.

Now, when the walls of Jerusalem were completed and all the gates had been rebuilt, the Jewish people who still lived in the area gathered in the Holy City for a dedication ceremony. During that ceremony, they read from the book of Deuteronomy the words of judgment against the Ammonites and the Moabites. Some of the people, in the intervening years, had intermarried with these heathen tribes, and they were now called upon to cleanse themselves.

But when Nehemiah went back to Persia, in his absence, backsliding set in immediately. One of the priests, a man named Eliashib, blatantly offended God by preparing Tobiah a special chamber in the temple. Now, suddenly, an Ammonite, a man who hated God and His people, was occupying a special place in the house of God. This happened because the priest got too close to a heathen man and made an unholy alliance with him.

If there's a sin in your life that you can't seem to get victory over, it's because you're too close to it and love it too much. You have invited what God has cursed to have a room in your life. Nothing can stay with you unless you make room for it. Again, the Scriptures declare that we're not to *"give place to the devil"* (Ephesians 4:27).

Men and women who sin eventually stop praying.

Eliashib didn't give Tobiah the main sanctuary of the temple. What he gave him was a small chamber. But even that was too much. Also, the room he gave Tobiah was an important one. It was a place where valuable offerings to God had been stored.

One of those offerings was frankincense, which represents the prayers of the saints. You're God's temple, but Satan is intent upon having within you a chamber reserved for an Ammonite. When you let him in, the first thing to suffer will be your prayer life.

Men and women who sin eventually stop praying. They may pretend to pray in public for a while, but because of the presence of sin in their lives, staying where God is will be painful for them.

This chamber given to a heathen man was also the place where grain offerings were stored, and these represent worship. Many Christians cannot worship in freedom because there's an Ammonite living in their house. His presence has displaced prayer, and it has displaced worship.

During worship times, they're not thinking of the omnipotence of God and the might and holiness of Jehovah. Rather, they're thinking things like:

"When will this all be over?"

"Do I look like I'm doing okay?"

"Am I faking it well enough?"

"Where should we eat today?"

"What should we do tonight?"

To them, it's all a show. They're trying to impress people. There's an Ammonite living in their house, and he has occupied an important chamber—the chamber of prayer and worship.

The chamber the Ammonite unlawfully occupied had also been used to store tithes and offerings. So the presence of the Ammonite affected the giving of the people, and that affected their daily needs. I hope you don't have any money in your bank account that belongs to God and that none of His money was invested in your car or your home. That would bring a curse upon your life.

If you have allowed an Ammonite to live in your house, God rejects your form of godliness. He said through the prophet Amos:

I hate, I despise your feast days, and I will not smell in your solemn assemblies. Though ye offer me burnt offerings and your meat offerings, I will not accept them: neither will I regard the peace offerings of your fat beasts. Take thou away from me the noise of thy songs; for I will not hear the melody of thy viols. But let judgment run down as waters, and righteousness as a mighty stream.

Amos 5:21-24

How terrible when God hates our every activity!

The chamber given to the Ammonite had also been used to store offerings of wine and oil, and these represent the very life of God's Spirit. Where evil reigns, He will not be found. At some point, He will be grieved and forced to retreat.

Today we seem to think that we're somehow special in this regard. We can do things that have been forbidden in the past, and now they're somehow okay. Even though we know that what we're doing is wrong, we're convinced that we're the exception to God's rule. We're His pet, and He won't get angry with us.

The devil plays on these feelings, insisting, "It's all right. Everyone does a little wrong. Nobody's perfect. We're all just sinners." But if an Ammonite has been given a space in your house, you have offended God, and your soul is in danger.

EVICT PRIDE AND LUST TODAY

Pride and lust will destroy you, and the church is full of them both. They're the roots of every evil:

For all that is in the world, the lust of the flesh, and the lust of the eyes, and the pride of life, is not of the Father, but is of the world. And the world passeth away, and the lust thereof: but he that doeth the will of God abideth for ever.

1 John 2:16-17

Why is it that we become proud because of what God has done for us? It's only by His grace. He has anointed you for a special task, but that doesn't mean that He'll put up with anything you want to do. He doesn't need you; you need Him.

The fact that so many Christians sin attests to the truth that they're somehow convinced that God will overlook their particular sin. But the Bible does not allow for any exceptions to the rule.

And no one sin is worse than another sin. The sin of pride is no different from the sin of murder. The sin of unbelief is no greater than the sin of adultery. It's all the same to God. Unbelief, self-pity, disobedience, murder, and any other sin all do the same thing. Sin—whatever sin—stops the work of God in your life. No matter how great or how small your sin is, it will stop what God wants to do with you and for you.

MOSES' MIRY PLACES

The tragedy of allowing sin into your life is graphically illustrated in the life of Moses. This man Moses was such a great man that only God occupies more space in the Bible than him.

Moses is mentioned twelve hundred times in the sacred Scriptures. He was a man who stood on holy ground and talked to God face-to-face. He witnessed his rod turned into a serpent. He learned the name of God when the Lord said to him, "I Am that I Am." Still, there was sin in Moses' life. As he started his journey to deliver the people of Israel from Egyptian bondage, the Bible says of him:

And it came to pass by the way in the inn, that the Lord met him and sought to kill him.

Exodus 4:24

Moses had just gotten to the Holiday Inn, had checked in, signing his VISA slip in the process, and had gone to his room and taken off his shoes so that he could relax a little, when the Lord appeared and tried to kill him. And, again, we're talking about one of the greatest men in the Bible.

What does all of this mean? It means that you will never reach a place in God that you can afford to overlook sin. God cannot overlook sin or allow you to overlook sin—even your own sin. You will never become so popular, so powerful, so useful, and so necessary that God will overlook your sin. So never succumb to the temptation of thinking that you're somehow the exception to God's rule.

Most Bible scholars believe that when God met Moses that day and tried to kill him it was because he had not circumcised his second son. His wife, Zipporah, was offended by the fact that God told the people to circumcise their children, so she opposed Moses in this matter, and he gave in to her.

I think we can imagine what Satan was saying to Moses about then. "This is such a small matter. Why not let her have her way this time? What will it hurt? You have a great mandate from God to deliver the people, and you don't need to be distracted by something as minor as this. Believe me, God will understand."

But in God's eyes, this was no small thing. Circumcision was part of a covenant God had made with Abraham and his descendants. The physical act of circumcision was a sign of separation between the followers of Jehovah and others, and Moses, as one of the major leaders of His people, could not be exempt.

Could Moses be sent to Egypt to enable the fulfillment of God's covenant with His people and, at the same time, not be a party to that covenant himself? Never! He needed to get his own house in order if he was to lead others.

God could have raised up anyone and sent them to deliver Israel. This was a privilege, and when Moses didn't appreciate it, God sought to take his life. He didn't need Moses. HE was the deliverer.

So the sin of omission nearly got Moses killed. What he did, disobeying God to try to keep peace in the family, may not seem like a very big sin to many, but God wouldn't permit it.

How is that a sin? Again, the Bible shows us: *"Therefore to him that knoweth to do good, and doeth it not, to him it is sin"* (James 4:17). The sin of omission is just disobedience in another form.

Some men are convinced that they're irreplaceable, and they can't imagine God doing His work without them. How foolish!

SIN'S INEVITABLE PAYDAY

It's true that God is loving, patient, and longsuffering, but there comes a time when His grace can no longer hold back the results of your sin. Before that time comes, He does everything He can to help you get your act together. But eventually He will have to step aside and allow the consequences of sin to take over. When this inevitably happens, it's payday:

> *The wages of sin is death; but the gift of God is eternal life through Jesus Christ our Lord.*
>
> Romans 6:23

In our pride, we often try to gloss over our wrongdoings. That's another reason God hates pride. Pride brings nothing but self-seeking and self-promoting. It fills men and women with ego, conceit, arrogance, jealousy, gossip, lying, and prejudice.

And the root of all racism is pride. Set aside your pride and deal with the sin that is in your life before it destroys you.

How can we read the Bible and not understand the consequences of sin? Consider, for instance, Adam and Eve; their disobedience cost them Paradise. Consider King Saul, the subject of the following chapter; he lost his throne. Consider Samson; he died a prisoner of the enemy. Consider Aaron's two sons; they were judged by God and burned up by His fire. Consider Eli and his two sons; they died in quick succession for their folly. Consider the people of the tribe of Korah; the ground opened up under them and swallowed them up alive. Consider the three thousand people who would not obey Moses in the wilderness; they were all destroyed. And the list goes on and on. It contains kings, priests, and prophets. You can't take the risk of living a life void of spiritual desire, a life given over to the lust of the flesh.

The minute Nehemiah got back to Jerusalem, he threw that Ammonite out of the temple and cleansed it. Then the first thing he did was to restore the oil and the wine representing the Holy Spirit. If He has left you, please don't waste any time in inviting him back to a your abode. But get the Ammonite out first, so God can have His rightful place in your life.

Nehemiah then restored the other offerings, the frankincense, the grain offerings and the meat offering. When sin has been removed, then restoration can take place.

Anytime we locate some sin, any sin, in our life, we need to get it out. It may be pride, lust, gossip, or bitterness. But, whatever it is, we need to identify it and get it out of there. Then allow the Holy Ghost to fumigate that place and then to refill us with His Spirit.

Pray, "God, refill me. I let an Ammonite into the house, but he's gone now. Take up Your rightful abode. I need You in my life."

It's time to lay aside every weight and the sin which does so easily beset us, and to run with patience the race that is set before us. And please leave no pagan altars standing. When any biblical leader left standing facilities dedicated to other gods, inevitably the people returned to their idolatry. Tear them all down. Get rid of them once and for all. If you give the devil any space at all, he'll attempt to rule your life again. Show God the intensity of your spiritual desire, and He will reward you handsomely.

If you're one of those people who are in a place where the river of God is flowing, but it's not touching you, you've allowed a miry place to remain in your life. Return to the love you had for the Lord when you were first saved. Start witnessing again and winning people to Him as you did when you felt that first blush of love. You were so excited then. Let that same excitement return and flood your soul today. There is an inseparable link between your desire and your destiny.

Chapter 8

SAUL'S SAD END: DESTINY LOST

Now go and smite Amalek, and utterly destroy all that they have, and spare them not; but slay both man and woman, infant and suckling, ox and sheep, camel and ass.

But Saul and the people spared Agag, and the best of the sheep, and of the oxen, and of the fatlings, and the lambs, and all that was good, and would not utterly destroy them: but every thing that was vile and refuse, that they destroyed utterly.

1 Samuel 15:3, 9

In God's Word, from Genesis to Revelation, obedience is the key to everything, but that obedience is possible only to those who are possessors of spiritual desire.

The biblical account of the early history of man begins with Adam's disobedience and moves on to Abraham's obedience. It contrasts Moses' disobedience with Joshua's obedience, Eli's disobedience with Samuel's obedience, and Saul's disobedience with David's obedience. That's just the beginning of the list, and it was all written as an example for us. In every chapter of His Word, God is trying to show us that it pays to obey Him, and it doesn't pay to disobey Him.

OBEDIENCE VS. DISOBEDIENCE

There is even an element of obedience necessary to our salvation. God said that we must believe with our hearts and confess with our mouths, and we have to do that to be saved.

He has promised to send His Spirit upon those who obey Him:

And we are his witnesses of these things; and so is also the Holy Ghost, whom God hath given to them that obey him.

Acts 5:32

Faith is revealed through obedience, for it is nothing more than obeying what God has said because we believe it. If we don't obey, it means that we don't really believe.

Throughout Paul's writings to the church, there are interspersed instructions to be obeyed, and the New Testament concludes with the powerful book of Revelation that declares:

Blessed is he that readeth, and they that hear the words of this prophecy, and keep those things which are written therein.

Revelation 1:3

Blessed is he that keepeth the sayings of the prophecy of this book.

Revelation 22:9

Blessed are they that do his commandments, that they may have right to the tree of life, and may enter in through the gates into the city. For without are dogs, and sorcerers, and whoremongers, and murderers, and idolaters, and whosoever loveth and maketh a lie.

Revelation 22:14-15

So from the beginning of the Bible to the end, all of God's promised blessings hinge upon our obedience to Him and His teachings, and our obedience to Him hinges upon maintaining our spiritual desire.

The small book that bears Jonah's name is totally dedicated to his life of obedience (sometimes learned the hard way).

Jesus also taught obedience:

And Jesus called a little child unto him, and set him in the midst of them, and said, Verily I say unto you, Except ye be converted, and become as little children, ye shall not enter into the kingdom of heaven. Whosoever therefore shall humble himself as this little child, the same is greatest in the kingdom of heaven. And whoso shall receive one such little child in my name receiveth me. But whoso shall offend one of these little ones which believe in me, it were better for him that a millstone were hanged about his neck, and that he were drowned in the depth of the sea.

Matthew 18:2-6

One of the characteristics of this word *humble* is to be obedient. Children obey their parents. At least, they used to, and they still should.

SAUL'S DISOBEDIENCE

The prophet Samuel recorded the entire story of this man Saul who became Israel's first king. He started out on the right track. He was anointed by God and could prophesy under God's power. But then, in time, disobedience came into his life. With that disobedience, came jealousy. Next, the jealousy turned to rage. The result was that the end of Saul, who had started out so well, was very sad.

When God's favor is upon us, that brings strong obligations on our part.

◆

At the beginning of this fifteenth chapter, as Samuel was preparing to convey to Saul God's instructions, he reminded Saul of how he had risen to such heights of power:

Samuel also said unto Saul, The Lord sent me to anoint thee to be king over his people, over Israel: now therefore hearken thou unto the voice of the words of the Lord.

1 Samuel 15:1

When God's favor is upon us, that brings strong obligations on our part. He doesn't give us His power just to use as we want. The more we have from Him, the more important it is to be obedient to Him in all things.

God now had a job for Saul to do, and He had a reason for telling him what he was about to tell him. God is God, and He doesn't have to state His reasons for telling us to do something, but in this case He graciously did:

Thus saith the Lord of hosts, I remember that which Amalek did to Israel, how he laid wait for him in the way, when he came up from Egypt.

1 Samuel 15:2

Now Saul had no excuse. God had told him what to do and why. It was up to him to obey.

The Amalekites had not wanted to allow the children of Israel to pass through their land, and they had tried to hire a prophet named Balaam to curse God's chosen ones. This was the reason for God's severity toward them, and who was Saul to question it?

SAUL'S DISOBEDIENCE IS COMPOUNDED BY LIES

The sad thing is that when Saul returned from his mission, he reported to Samuel that he had done all that God required of him:

And Samuel came to Saul: and Saul said unto him, Blessed be thou of the Lord: I have performed the commandment of the Lord.

1 Samuel 15:13

This, of course, was not true, and God had already told Samuel that He was sorry He had made Saul king. Saul was bold enough in his disobedience to think that he could fool the prophet, but Samuel now asked the haughty king:

What meaneth then this bleating of the sheep in mine ears, and the lowing of the oxen which I hear?

1 Samuel 15:14

God wasn't fooled and neither was Samuel, and he let that be known. Some might think that the prophet's duty to respect and admire his king should have overridden any sense of disappointment he felt in Saul's duplicity, but even a king cannot disobey God and be free of consequences.

WHAT CAUSES DISOBEDIENCE IN BELIEVERS?

This is not to say that Saul didn't love the Lord in some capacity. He had not abandoned his faith in God. But the desires of his flesh had been allowed to take precedence over the will of God, and that could not stand.

Then, in pride, he did not want to give up his profession, but the reality of his life testified against him. The love of the world and the love of the Lord don't mix. God's Word declares:

Love not the world, neither the things that are in the world. If any man love the world, the love of the Father is not in him.

1 John 2:15-16

The animals that trailed after Saul and the sounds coming from them spoke louder than his protestations of innocence. And God was angry with him.

Saul was the king, but that didn't matter. Clearly it's not enough to have been saved for years or to have done great things for God's kingdom. He demands obedience today of each and every one of us if we're to claim Him as Lord of our lives.

Saul was quick to blame others and, thus, to excuse his own participation in the wrongdoing. "So-and-So did it" or "So-and-So made me do it" have been common justifications since the beginning of time. They haven't worked until now, and they won't work in the future. God holds every man and woman accountable for his or her own deeds.

Next, Saul tried two more excuses: that he had done most of what the Lord had commanded and that what he had not done was because he had a better plan:

> *And Saul said, They have brought them from the Amalekites: for the people spared the best of the sheep and of the oxen, to sacrifice unto the Lord thy God; and the rest we have utterly destroyed.*
>
> 1 Samuel 15:15

So Saul had obeyed in part, and in what part he had not obeyed, his intention had been good. He wanted to use those sheep and oxen to make a sacrifice to God. What could possibly be wrong with that?

GOD'S VERDICT ON SAUL'S DISOBEDIENCE

Samuel's answer to this good-sounding excuse is revealing. He reminded Saul again that when he had been little in his own sight, God had raised him up. Then, when he had been exalted and made king, God had given him a very explicit order. It could not have been misunderstood, and yet Saul had not obeyed it. Samuel refused to accept what Saul had done as being good in any way. Rather, he described it as *"evil in the sight of the* LORD*"* (verse 19).

Amazingly, Saul continued to assert his innocence, and he repeated the whole story. He had done exactly what the Lord had told him, but the people had insisted on keeping certain animals to sacrifice to God. To this, Samuel responded with words that have rung out down through the centuries:

Hath the Lord as great delight in burnt offerings and sacrifices, as in obeying the voice of the Lord? Behold, to obey is better than sacrifice, and to hearken than the fat of rams.

1 Samuel 15:22

Nothing can replace obedience. Nothing!

The context of this verse is very interesting. The sacrifices of the Old Testament were an integral part of the worship to God. So it is showing us that God doesn't welcome our worship if and when we're not willing to be obedient to Him.

Samuel went on to make his point even more forcefully:

For rebellion is as the sin of witchcraft, and stubbornness is as iniquity and idolatry.

1 Samuel 15:23

When Saul placed his will in direct competition to God's will and insisted again and again that he had done the right thing, he entered into open rebellion against the Almighty. It's one thing to make a mistake, but it's something else entirely to directly and intentionally disobey God, flaunt it, and think that we can get away with it. Do we dare enter into competition with the God of the universe?

Nothing can replace obedience. Nothing!

Witchcraft! Rebellion! Idolatry! Was Samuel using words that were much too strong? Not at all. This was a serious sin, and the consequences Samuel was about to announce would show just how serious a sin it really was in God's sight:

162

Because thou hast rejected the word of the Lord, he hath also rejected thee from being king.

1 Samuel 15:23

The attitude of so many today is: "I don't care what you show me in the Bible. I know what I want, and I know what I believe, and I'm sure that God understands." Well, you'd better care, because the consequences of direct disobedience to God are serious for anyone. Saul lost his kingdom.

WAS SAUL'S PUNISHMENT TOO HARSH?

Was it too harsh a reaction to remove Saul from his throne for this infraction? God didn't think so. If we're not submitted to Him, then He can't require others to be submitted to us. Only those who are fully submitted to God are worthy to rule in His kingdom.

Just that quickly the kingdom was ripped from Saul's hands. He would remain at his post for some time, but he was just a shell of the former man God had made him. Jesus said:

If ye love me, keep my commandments.

John 14:15

This people draweth nigh unto me with their mouth, and honoureth me with their lips; but their heart is far from me. But in vain they do worship me, teaching for doctrines the commandments of men.

Matthew 15:8-9

God wants not only words of love from us, but He is also calling for a demonstration of our love. If you love Him, show it. Prove your love by obeying Him.

Is it logical or believable when someone says, "I love you," and then treats you badly? It doesn't convince me, and it doesn't convince God either.

WHAT IS "PRESUMPTUOUS SIN"?

Men who act as Saul did are being presumptuous with God. David spoke of *"presumptuous sins"*:

Keep back thy servant also from presumptuous sins; let them not have dominion over me: then shall I be upright, and I shall be innocent from the great transgression.

Psalm 19:13

What did David mean by *"presumptuous sins"*? According to *Webster's Dictionary,* the meaning of *presumptuous* is "overstepping due bounds (as of propriety or courtesy): taking liberties." You can't afford to take liberties with God. If He forbids a thing, then you can't approve it. And if He approves a thing, then you can't forbid it.

Don't make the mistake of thinking that you'll be forgiven just because Mamma was a missionary or Daddy was a pastor. You may have been raised in the church, and God may know that you have always loved Him, but that doesn't give you the right to break His laws. What makes you think that you'll get by when others have not? You may be the apple of God's eye, but when you start setting your will up against His, you're in trouble. This is the sin of presumption, and it will not go unpunished.

Who are you to put your opinions and feelings up against God's Holy Word? You may not be able to see how a God of love could punish people, but you'll soon learn if you continue to flaunt His laws.

GOD NOW DEMANDS REPENTANCE

The two sons of Aaron, who served as high priests during the time of Moses, presumed that because they were trained for the ministry of the wilderness tabernacle and ordained by God precisely for that purpose, they could do no wrong. He had told them not to use any fire but the fire He provided, and they understood this. Still, for some strange reason, they presumed that they could experiment with the fire of the tabernacle and that no harm would come to them. They were wrong. Their presumption brought them sudden death, and that should be a lesson to us all.

There was a time when *"God winked at"* ignorance. Indeed, during Old Testament times, the priests made sacrifice for the people for having sinned in ignorance. But this changed with the coming of Jesus. God's Word now tells us:

And the times of this ignorance God winked at; but now commandeth all men every where to repent: because he hath appointed a day, in the which he will judge the world in righteousness by that man whom he hath ordained; whereof he hath given assurance unto all men, in that he hath raised him from the dead.

Acts 17:30-31

SAMSON'S PRESUMPTION

Samson was another great man who became presumptuous. All of his life he had heard his mamma tell the story of the angel who appeared to her and told her that she was to have a son, and that this son was to be very special in God's sight. As a sign of his specialness, a razor would never be allowed to touch this child's head. In time, he would become a deliverer for his people. "You're destined to be very powerful, my son," she would say to him often.

Samson had heard his father tell a similar story. When his wife told him about the angel she had seen and what he had said, he wanted to hear it for himself. Sure enough, an angel came to him presently and told him the exact same thing. Their son would be very special and would grow up to be a great servant of God.

In the years to come, Samson's parents did what was required of them. They protected their son and kept him separated for the chosen work he would someday be called upon to do. But they also must have been guilty of spoiling their son terribly, because by the time he was grown, a certain pride had set into his spirit, and he possessed a certain crassness with regard to God's will for his life. He was not nearly as careful to protect himself from contamination as his parents had been in protecting him until then.

When Samson was tempted to seek pleasure with the Philistine women, he just couldn't believe that this would matter to God. After all, he was the chosen deliverer of Israel. Surely God would overlook his momentary indiscretions. But one indiscretion led to another ... until the man whose birth had been announced by angels was found with his head in the lap of the devil.

And that was not the end of it. Before long, God's champion had become nothing more than a bald-headed clown. He had once been highly respected, but he was now a laughing stock among the hated Philistines.

THAT'S NOT ME

I'm sure most of you who are reading this book will not see yourselves in this picture. You'll say, "That's not me." But if you're trying to find ways around the things God has spoken to you, you're just as guilty as Samson. You have grown cold and lost your "first love."

Surely God would not judge you, you reason. After all, you go to church, you pay your tithes, and you're obedient to God's dictates in most things. But is there an Amalekite in your life? An Ammonite? Is there some miry clay that you're holding onto?

> *Stop trying to make God something that He's not.*

Please don't be guilty of the sin of presumption. Others thought they could get by with halfhearted service to God, but He didn't see their "little" sin as little, and He judged them.

"Men are just men," Samson must have said to himself, but lustful desires will take any man or any woman to hell. If the love of the world is in you, it means that the love of the Father has departed. And that's very dangerous.

WHAT IS IDOLATRY?

To most of us, idolatry is the overt act of bowing the knee before some graven image, some other god. But, in reality, it's much more than that. If we imagine certain things about God and then act like they're so, that's as much idolatry as the overt act of bowing the knee to false gods.

Stop trying to make God something that He's not. You have no right to do that. You have no right to imagine anything at all about God. He has given us His Word, and it tells us everything He wants us to know about Him. To make Him anything other than what the Bible says He is, is the worst kind of sin one could possibly commit.

God deliver us from thinking that just because we're anointed by Him it means that we don't have to play by His rules. Yes, we're His special children, but we're special only because He is with us. If we choose to leave Him, that specialness will depart with Him.

As children of God, we all know that periodically God deals with us about things in our lives that are not pleasing to Him. If we fail to quickly and willingly rid ourselves of these obstacles to His love, this says to Him that we assume that He's going to allow us to get by with whatever we're doing that He's not happy with. That's the kind of pride that goes before destruction and a fall:

Pride goeth before destruction, and an haughty spirit before a fall.

Proverbs 16:18

If your love for God has grown cold, please let His Spirit renew you today. Don't risk eternity without the Father.

JUDGMENT DELAYED

Often God's judgment is delayed, and we think we have gotten away with some evil deed. But the longer His judgment is delayed, the more severe the punishment will be when it does come. Just because we're not immediately executed doesn't mean that we're safe from punishment. God's judgment for sin is sure. Like a bloodhound from hell, it will find you wherever you happen to be.

Sometimes it may seem that you're doing well, but, as we saw in the last chapter, there will come a moment in which the Holy Spirit will step aside and allow judgment to flood in upon you. "I've done all that I can do," He'll have to say. "I have wooed you and convicted you. I tried to get your conscience to set off alarm bells inside of you. I tried everything I knew to try, but you haven't heeded." Then the Holy Ghost has to withdraw His presence and allow you to become fair game for the devil.

When your sins finally catch up to you, don't expect others to bear the consequences. *"Your sin will find YOU out"* (Numbers 32:23).

A PATTERN OF DISOBEDIENCE

There's a pattern to be found throughout the Bible that seems to be repeated all too often in modern life. A prophet (maybe a pastor in modern terms) comes our way and preaches the Word of God. We're "turned on" by it, and our hearts are stirred so that we make a public commitment to forsake sin and serve God.

I've watched it happen thousands of times in altars across the world. "God, I'm going to straighten my life out and get my act together. I'll forsake every sin, and I'll start doing something meaningful for You. You can depend on me, Lord. Use me."

But strangely, within a very short time, many of those who have uttered such sincere-sounding pledges have forgotten their words of commitment. What has happened? I'm convinced that people are sincere when they pray, but they make a fatal mistake in not allowing total change to come to their lives. They leave an Ammonite in their house and don't clean it out fully, and the result is that they soon go back to the same life as before.

Those sacred moments at the altar turn out to be just a little prayer that was prayed with no meaningful follow-up, and no real lasting commitment. Oh, they plan to go to church—when it's convenient to do so—and to tithe—when they can afford it, but, because there's no lasting change, there will be little fruit.

Being moved by the Spirit of God is not wrong. That's a good beginning. Making a commitment to God is not wrong. We all need to do it. But these must be followed by meaningful changes in our everyday life so that we can truly become soldiers of the cross.

One Wednesday night some months ago, we had more than a hundred people standing at our altar expressing a desire to be used by God. I had told them not to come forward if they were not serious about it, and still they came.

We took time to tell these people how they could become involved in the various ministries of the church, and a few weeks later I asked the leaders of those ministries if they had received any concrete help from that group. One person had approached the leaders to say that he or she wanted to help with the children's ministries, and a few others had expressed a desire to help with outreach ministries. That was as far as it went.

People get stirred up, and they're on fire for a week or two, and then they forget it. If we begin a new prayer ministry with fifty willing souls, the next week only twenty show up, and the next week we have only five. And that's just the way it is these days.

Every time a new leader came to the throne in Israel, he would call for a cleansing of the temple. He would call for the high places dedicated to idols to be torn down, and then he would bring back the worship of the true God.

In these moments, all of Israel would rejoice. They had come back to God, and He had come back to them. But invariably they left a few of the high places standing, and this resulted in a diluted faith, a partial obedience, and eventual backsliding. Those high places called to the people and drew them until they again forsook the house of God and went after other gods.

The devil doesn't need much room to insert a wedge into your life. God's Word advises us: *"Neither give place to the devil"* (Ephesians 4:27). We're not to give him a place, because when he has found even a small place, he works tirelessly to enlarge it. If you leave a little bit of temper, a little bit of bitterness, or a little bit of unforgiveness, that's all he needs in order to slowly take control of you. If you give him his place, he'll allow you to go to church, pay your tithes, and even speak in tongues once in a while. He's satisfied with the little place you've given him, and he knows that eventually he will control you totally.

As we have noted previously in the book, John wrote to the church:

For all that is in the world, the lust of the flesh, and the lust of the eyes, and the pride of life, is not of the Father, but is of the world. And the world passeth away, and the lust thereof: but he that doeth the will of God abideth for ever.

1 John 2:16-17

These two elements, pride and lust, are the things most believers have to deal with. These are the besetting sins of our day.

Pride is thinking more highly of yourself than you should:

For I say, through the grace given unto me, to every man that is among you, not to think of himself more highly than he ought to think; but to think soberly, according as God hath dealt to every man the measure of faith.

Romans 12:3

Pride thirsts after honor and the applause of men. God blesses us with gifts and lends us His anointing, but we must never come to believe that what results has been done by our own might. It's never, "I've done something wonderful!" Rather, it's, "He's done everything that's wonderful." Falling in love with Jesus will cure all pride.

At home I have a little Jesus corner, and there I keep a painting that I love. It's of a small girl. She has on her mother's dress and her father's shoes, and she's trying to hold up the dress so that she can walk in those big shoes. Every morning and every night that I'm home, I get down on my knees beside that painting, and I say, "God, that's me. That's how I feel with Your mantle on me. Help me never to lose that sense of awe at my smallness and Your greatness."

That's exactly what happened to Saul. As long as he was small in his own eyes, he was fine. But just as soon as he decided that he somehow deserved to be king, then God had to bring him down.

Lust, in one form or another, seems to be the besetting sin for most people of our age. More people are destroyed by it than by any other temptation.

"The lust of the flesh" of which the Scriptures speak is a craving for fleshly desires and pleasures. These might be sexual pleasures, but they could also be for something that we consider to be just fun and games.

"The lust of the eye" of which the Scriptures speak is covetousness, wanting something that doesn't belong to you. And

if it doesn't belong to you, it's also something you don't need. It might be a serious craving for a bigger house, a better car, or enough money to be considered independently wealthy.

It seems to be an obsession of our generation to work hard and accumulate as much as possible in life, almost as if there were some prize for the person who has left behind the most toys. Life is short, we rationalize, and so we need to experience as much of it as possible as quickly as possible. But life is not a contest, and things are not the treasures we should be seeking.

REPENTANCE FROM SIN SPARKS REVIVAL

Evan Roberts, the great Welsh revivalist, left us a powerful testimony about how revival begins. Today we consider that the most important elements of revival are great advertising and great organization. But, although "come and get your miracle" and "come and see the man of God who will bring you healing" may be interesting slogans, they could never produce revival. There may indeed be miracles, and people may be saved and blessed, but true revival always starts with a small group of people who have purified themselves.

After he had fasted and prayed for many days, Evan Roberts went to church one night with a message from God. The crowd that night consisted of just seventeen people, and the message he had for them consisted of three things that they should do: (1) They should lay aside every habit that was displeasing to God, (2) They should confess every known sin in their lives, and (3) They should make things right with every human being they had wronged.

This was God's recipe for revival, and the people accepted it. Within the first twenty-four hours, more than thirty thousand people had been touched by the revival, and within a short time, the whole world had to sit up and take notice of what God was doing in Wales.

WHY DOESN'T REVIVAL COME TO US?

What's wrong with us today? Why doesn't revival come? Personally, I'm convinced that it's because we have some miry places in our lives. We have some Amalekite still occupying space in our home. There's something that we need to get rid of. And we all need to start obeying the Word of God. Disobedience to God might not always kill you outrightly, but it will surely contaminate your soul and prevent you from going deeper in God.

Revival is not just getting happy, shaking, quaking, and falling on the floor. That may be a part of it, but that alone is not enough.

Revival, when it comes, will do a lot more than make you laugh or giggle like you're drunk. That may be part of it too, but true revival will touch every part of your community. It will send you outside the church walls with a message about what's happening in your life. And many others will be blessed as a result.

Why would any of us risk spoiling God's desire for revival among us? I, for one, don't want to be guilty of doing anything that would hinder revival. I have been asking God to show me anything that I have done in ignorance that does not please Him, so that I can change.

If God shows me something, anything, that does not please Him, I want to get it out of my life, and I want to get it out of my life now. I beg for God's forgiveness, and I vow to change fully. I don't want anything in me to hinder the move of God in the earth.

It's time to confess and forsake anything that hinders and to make it right. Remove all of the Ammonites. Stir up the miry places. Cause the stagnant waters to come forth and get those parts of your life into the river so that you can be healed. Say to God today, "Whatever it takes, let my will be broken, so that I can be one with You."

In short, let Him renew your first love and cause to flame again the ebbing embers of your soul. There is an inseparable link between your desire and your destiny.

Chapter 9

GOD IS WAITING TO HEAR YOUR PRAISE

Praise him for his mighty acts: praise him according to his excellent greatness.

Psalm 150:2

Desire determines the intensity of your worship to God, just as it does the intensity of your relationship to any other person. That's why God is waiting to hear your praise.

HE'S CALLING FOR YOUR EXPRESSIONS OF LOVE

His Word admonishes us to praise Him for His mighty acts, to praise Him according to His excellent greatness. He knows it all, but He wants to hear you say it. He wants to hear your words of love.

"Tell Me," He's saying. "Let Me hear it. Praise Me for delivering Daniel from the lion's den. Praise Me for what I did for the three Hebrew boys in the fiery furnace. Praise Me for what happened at the Red Sea. Tell Me. I want to hear your voice of praise."

Each of us likes to be praised, and that's because we were made in God's image. We were created to *"show forth the praises of the Lord"*:

They shall show forth the praises of the Lord.

Isaiah 60:6

But ye are a chosen generation, a royal priesthood, an holy nation, a peculiar people; that ye should show forth the praises of him who hath called you out of darkness into his marvellous light.

1 Peter 2:9

We all know what it feels like to have someone bragging on us. A great smile comes over our faces, we throw back our shoulders, and we're ready to take on a lion. That's how David felt one day. He said:

For by thee I have run through a troop: by my God have I leaped over a wall.

2 Samuel 22:30

Praise, more than anything else, will turn your life around and set you on a path toward victory.

God knows that He's good, but He wants to hear you say it anyway. He's no egomaniac, but He has chosen to dwell in the praises of His people.

Yes, God lives in praise. He's just got to have it. And He declared that if we don't praise Him, rocks will cry out:

And when he was come nigh, even now at the descent of the mount of Olives, the whole multitude of the disciples began to rejoice and praise God with a loud voice for all the mighty works that they had seen; saying, Blessed be the King that cometh in the name of the Lord: peace in heaven, and glory in the highest. And some of the Pharisees from among the multitude said unto him, Master, rebuke thy disciples. And he answered and said unto them, I tell you that, if these should hold their peace, the stones would immediately cry out.

Luke 19:37-40

If you want to meet with God, you have to come to Him through gates of thanksgiving. That's where He lives. You cannot come to Him without passing through courts of praise:

Enter into his gates with thanksgiving, and into his courts with praise: be thankful unto him, and bless his name.

Psalm 100:4

If you learn to come to God in this way, you will be welcomed inside His most intimate sanctuary every time. He wants to grant you access to His throne room, to give you the very keys to His kingdom. Your praise speaks to Him of your love, and your love unlocks to you all of the treasures of heaven.

Lawrence and I decided to put a combination lock on our back door, and we gave the combination to a few people we were close to, people we knew we could trust. Do you realize that God has given you the combination to His door? Thanksgiving, praise, and worship ... these are the keys that give you access to God at any time and anywhere. WOW! That's powerful!

HIS WILL IS THAT THERE BE
MUTUAL EXPRESSIONS OF LOVE

God not only longs for your expressions of love to Him; He makes it mutual. He whispers words of love into your heart too.

Do you say "good night" and "good morning" to everyone else but God?

If two people wanted to form a friendship, but it wasn't clear that they valued each other's worth, how could any meaningful relationship be developed? The Lord will always make known to you how very much He loves you, and then He's waiting to hear that you appreciate Him too.

What's He worth to you? What do you think of Him? Has He been good to you? Tell Him, and you can have anything He has. Prayerlessness has robbed you of many blessings. Don't let that stand even one more day.

We should be thanking God every day for our health and strength, for the means of supporting ourselves, for friends and family, for everything we have in this life.

Do you say "good night" and "good morning" to everyone else but God? Greeting Him as you do anyone else would be a good beginning to a life of sweet communion. But that's just the beginning. Don't stop there.

In true prayer, you think of His goodness and what He's done for you, and your heart wants to leap out of you for the joy of it all. You think about where you used to be and where you could be, and you want to thank Him for where you are today.

There was a time when you had no car, and you didn't know where you would live. And just look at you now. You have a house, a car, and a job. Look what the Lord has done! Get excited about it!

The devil doesn't want you to think about those things, and he does all within his power to keep your mind cluttered and confused. Rather than think about where you used to be and where you might have been, he wants to make you dissatisfied with where you are today.

He surely doesn't want you to remember that you were on your way to hell when God sent an angel and turned you around. He doesn't want you to remember the pit you were in before God picked you up and put you on the Solid Rock.

No, he doesn't want you to be thankful to God or have time to praise Him. He wants to keep you focused on your current problems and how you're going to get out of them, so that you'll forget that if God did it once, then He can do it again.

The devil doesn't want you to start praising God. He knows that if you start praising Him, you'll unlock the windows of heaven over your life, and God will look down from heaven and say, "What do you need from Me today, My child? Just name it, and it's yours."

Praise, the language of love between two people who simply can't live without each other, is powerful and life-changing. Let it start and end your day today, and even let if fill the hours in between. There is an inseparable link between your desire and your destiny.